Coalescent Argumentation

LEA TITLES IN ARGUMENTATION

Gilbert • Coalescent Argumentation

Walton • Argumentation Schemes for Presumptive Reasoning

van Eemeren et al. • Fundamentals of Argumentation Theory:
A Handbook of Historical Backgrounds and Contemporary
Developments

(Frans van Eemeren/Rob Grootendorst, Advisors)

van Eemeren/Grootendorst • Argumentation, Communication,
and Fallacies: A Pragma-Dialectical Perspective

Coalescent Argumentation

Michael A. Gilbert
York University

LEA LAWRENCE ERLBAUM ASSOCIATES, PUBLISHERS
1997   Mahwah, New Jersey

Lawrence Erlbaum Associates, Inc., Publishers
10 Industrial Avenue
Mahwah, NJ 07430

Cover design by Jan Melchior

Library of Congress Cataloging-in-Publication Data

Gilbert, Michael A.
      Coalescent Argumentation / by Michael A. Gilbert
            p. cm.
      Some chapters are revisions of articles previously pub-
lished in other sources, 1994–1995.
      Includes bibliographic references and index.
      ISBN 0-8058-2519-3 (c : alk. paper). — ISBN 0-8058-
2520-7 (p : alk. paper)
      1. Persuasion (Rhetoric)   I. Title.
      P301.5.P47G55   1997
      808—dc20   96-32875
                                                       CIP

Books published by Lawrence Erlbaum Associates are printed
on acid-free paper, and their bindings are chosen for strength
and durability.

10   9   8   7   6   5   4   3   2   1

For my brother,

Gary Gilbert,

and my sister,

Debbi Brantz,

for always teaching me and always loving me,

then as now.

Contents

Part I   Argumentation Theory

Part II   Multi-Modal Argumentation

List of Tables and Figures

List of Examples

Preface

Argument is one of the most common, useful, and dangerous of human communicative practices. It is done frequently—daily or hourly, by virtually everyone. Without it we would be incapable of changing our minds, advancing knowledge, or exploring the deeper issues involved in our agreement or disagreement. But, as important as argument is, it often goes wrong, and frequently the most common approaches emphasize opposition and the identification of the participants as opponents. This leads to forms of argument that are primarily designed to alter a dispute partner's point of view rather than uncover deeper and more meaningful issues.

I have, for a long time, felt there were other, more creative and cooperative approaches to argumentation that could better serve everyday arguers. This book presents the major aspects of such an approach. It involves the presentation of a system that first, accepts that people argue in ways that are not strictly logical; secondly, treats goals involved in argumentation as both manifold and important; and, finally, presents a mode of argumentation that is based on agreement rather than criticism. The aim, ultimately, is to bring together or *coalesce,* diverse positions so that the goal satisfaction of both participants can be maximized.

The first part of the book lays the foundations for the second. Chapter 1 is an overview of recent developments in Argumentation Theory. This chapter is introductory in nature and will acquaint the student or professional not familiar with Argumentation Theory with the dramatic growth and change in that area. Chapter 2 addresses the question of how the term 'argument' ought to be construed. Should it be considered a narrow technical notion, or should it be given a broad construction? A version of this chapter originally appeared in *Inquiry*, under the same title in 1995. Chapter 3 addresses itself to the field of Critical Thinking and how that area has approached argumentation. I identify a number of deficiencies that my approach aims to repair. This chapter first appeared in an altered form in *Teaching Philosophy* in 1995. Chapter 4 concerns the impact feminist theory has had, or, perhaps more correctly, *should have*, on Argumentation Theory. I address the concerns expressed by several feminist thinkers and incorporate what I take to be many of the underlying values into my approach. A version of this chapter appeared under the same title in *Informal Logic*, also in 1995.

Chapter 5 begins the positive elaboration of my theory by presenting a discussion of the relationship of goals, and, in particular, the invariably diverse and manifold nature of goals, to everyday argumentation. Chapter 6, which is adapted from an article of the same name that appeared in *Philosophy of the Social Sciences* in 1994 presents the essential metaphysics of my approach, and argues for the diverse sense of rationality I favor. The subsequent chapter discusses the detailed impact of multi-modal argumentation on Argumentation Theory, and provides examples its effects. Chapter 8 is adapted from "Coalescent Argumentation," which appeared in the journal Argumentation, and is used with the kind permission of Kluwer Academic. In that chapter I present the heart of the theory of agreement-based argumentation. The following chapter expands on this theme and presents a number of examples to exemplify the method. Finally, in chapter 10, I deal with some of the more obvious criticisms and questions, and make some concluding remarks.

Acknowledgments

The material presented here is controversial. There are many people in the field who have disagreed with me, taken issue with fundamental points, and baldly declared me wrong. They claim that rationality is and must be essentially logical, that every mode of argument I identify as diverse can be reduced to the logico-linear mode, and that argument must be critical in order to avoid error and self-deception. Nonetheless, through many fine and sometimes heated discussions on these issues, most of my colleagues in Argumentation Theory have come to understand where I am going and see my vision. While this has not always entailed subsequent agreement, their criticisms and arguments have sharpened my own understanding of my views as well as theirs, and for this I thank them.

This work has received financial support from a number of sources. I want to thank the Social Sciences and Humanities Research Council and York University for funding that permitted me to attend a number of valuable conferences as well as contributing to my residences in Amsterdam and Los Angeles. Thanks go to the Instituut voor Neerlandistiek of the University of Amsterdam for office space, funding, and fine colleagues during my residence there in September 1995. I also want to extend my gratitude to the University of Southern California where I was a Scholar in Residence, sponsored by the Center for Feminist Research and the Program for the Study of Women and Men in Society.

The Argumentation Theory community is a grand one, mutually supportive and highly constructive in its approach to criticism even when disagreements are profound. I am indebted to the many fine scholars I have encountered at conferences in North America and Europe. I am especially fortunate to have an active community of scholars in southern Ontario who uniformly embody the finest principles of argumentation.

The controversial nature of my writing has meant that the road was anything but easy. Individual thanks are due to a number of people who have supported me and urged me on when my personal doubts were deepest. Ralph Johnson, although there is much he disagrees with, has consistently offered encouragement and friendship for which I am thankful. Closer to home, Les Green and Claudio Duran of York University have regularly assured me that there is method to my madness. Also at York is my hard-working and indefatigable research assistant, David Godden, whose contributions to drafts have been valuable and insightful. I take pleasure in expressing my great appreciation for the time, wisdom, and friendship given me by Frans van Eemeren and Rob Grootendorst while I was in Amsterdam. Our discussions contributed greatly to anything of value in this book.

A special thanks goes to Charlie Willard, a stunning thinker and major influence in my thinking. It was Charlie who first urged me to go public and get serious about getting my views known. Without that push, this book and the papers on which it is based may not have been written.

Finally, my thanks and love to my wife Diane who never once doubted that I had something important to say and always believed, even when I did not, that others would listen.

Even having had so much help and encouragement, every mistake, error, wrong turning, and calumny in this book is all mine. I just hope there are not too many, and that the reader will be able to see beyond the disagreements to the shared goals that lay beneath the surface.

Michael A. Gilbert
Toronto, Canada

Part I

Argumentation Theory

1

The Recent History of Argumentation Theory

Although this chapter may be of interest to all readers, it is particularly intended to assist those who do not have a thorough familiarity with contemporary Argumentation Theory.

Philosophy has had an intimate connection to argument since ancient times. The philosopher, after all, rarely has recourse to the tools and experiments used in the physical and social sciences. One does not usually defend a particular philosophical theory or approach by empirical research, and use of the "actual" world is most often confined to *gedanken* experiments. Rather, philosophers use argument to determine if a position has flaws and weaknesses, and we expect that the loser in a philosophical argument will abandon his or her position or, (perhaps more realistically), withdraw from the field to effect repairs. Perhaps as a result of the reliance of philosophy on argumentation, philosophers have always had a tremendous respect for its importance as well as a strong sense of responsibility to both its formal and informal study and its pedagogical propagation.

There has been, since Aristotle's time, two basic ways to study argumentation in the domain of philosophy. The first way is formal, and utilizes the models of deductive logic. The second way, which like the first can be traced back to Aristotle (and before), is practical and has come to be called 'Informal Logic' or 'critical thinking' or some similar rubric. In recent times, however, dramatic changes have taken place in the kind of work being done on argumentation, so that we can now say that a virtually new field has been created on the older foundations. Called *Argumentation Theory*, this new arena of scholarly pursuit has its contemporary roots back in the 1950s, but only recently has assumed a shape that is sufficiently definable so as to be considered a (relatively) independent sub-area of endeavor. In addition to formal deductive logic and critical thinking, Argumentation Theory draws upon formal dialogue theory, the philosophy of language (especially in the form of speech act theory), Communication Theory, Discourse Analysis, and several areas of Psychology. The hallmarks that set argumentation theory apart from

3

its predecessors are two: The first is a strong emphasis on dialogical argumentation, i.e., two persons having an argument, rather than the traditional single person encountering a bit of text. The second is that argumentation theorists more and more view arguments as *situated* or taking place in a locatable context that itself is liable to have an impact on both the arguments and arguers.

The goal here is to describe the recent history of the field and lay out the several distinct approaches within philosophy and other disciplines that are tending more and more to intertwine and slowly evolve toward a more unified approach. These approaches include, among other things, an unusual degree of reliance on various branches of the Social Sciences as well as work in European philosophical circles. More emphasis, therefore, will be laid on scholars who are liable to be less familiar to the reader. I hope to demonstrate the renewed vitality of Argumentation Theory, and encourage other scholars to become aware of the connections their own work might have to this area.

While virtually all the roots of contemporary formal and informal logic go back to Aristotle, these will not be reviewed here. There is, however, one distinction he introduced that is crucial to this study, and that is the distinction between *dialectic* and *rhetoric*. The former seeks out truth by using logic and reasoning, whereas the latter uses persuasion and emotion to influence an audience's mind. Aristotle did not actually see the differences as being very sharp, but he did separate the areas by creating different realms of study for each. This subsequently led other scholars to harden the distinction, very likely to a degree Aristotle would not have accepted. At all events, the distinction has had a profound impact on the history of logic and argumentation, and has undergirded what is sometimes called the *convince/persuade dichotomy*. According to this distinction, to convince is to use reason, dialectic and logic, while to persuade is to rely on emotion, prejudice, and language. This distinction has moral as well as logical implications insofar as "convincing" has been considered to be a superior method. "Persuading" appeals to the "baser" components of the human psyche, namely, the emotions, while 'convincing' speaks to the "higher" aspects, namely, reason. On this view, one who is persuaded may be so for reasons that have little to do with the value of the arguments or the truth of the premises put forward.

Hand in hand with this distinction is the further subdivision of rhetoric by Aristotle into three separate areas: *logos, ethos,* and *pathos*. The result of Aristotle's dividing rhetoric into these three aspects has been the assumption that the areas can be dealt with as separate fields, each of which concerns argumentation in a very different but unrelated way. As a result, three distinct areas developed in virtual independence of each other. Formal Logic (logos) focused on the structural aspects of arguments, and, in particular, on the articulation and (to some) excruciatingly exact amplification of the concept of formal validity. Ethos, insofar as it was accorded any concern at all by philosophers, became a part of Informal Logic found in such notions as the *argumentums ad hominem, misericordiam,* and *vericundiam*. Pathos, or emotionality, which Aristotle viewed as central to rhetoric, was given even less attention. Certainly, one has several fallacies that, like those linked to ethos, can be seen as somehow connected to pathos, but the stretch is even greater (see Walton, 1992, for discussions of this issue).

Not every discipline ignored the non-formal categories of ethos and pathos. Classical and modern rhetoric remained concerned with ethos and its impact on speechmaking. Pathos, on the other hand, was subsumed by psychology, and later taken up by communication theory. For philosophers, however, these two aspects of Aristotle's work were primarily seen as not relevant to the construction of good, sound, convincing arguments. It was not that philosophers believed that ethos and pathos had no impact on the acceptance and rejection of arguments, but rather they seemed to believe that these factors *ought* not have an impact. In other words, one ought to accept and reject arguments on the basis of logos alone. It is important to note the implicit assumption that logos can exist alone, independently of ethos and pathos. This essentially undefended axiom is central to the traditional philosophical approach to informal logic, and it has stood, more or less unquestioned until the relatively recent times to which we now turn.[1]

Perelman's New Rhetoric

There are two scholars generally considered to be the founders of contemporary Argumentation Theory, especially as it is understood in North America. The first is the Belgian argumentation theorist and jurisprude, Chaim Perelman, the second is the English philosopher Stephen Toulmin. In an amazing example of synchronicity, both of their seminal works were originally published in almost the same year. Perelman first published *The New Rhetoric*, L. Olbrechts-Tyteca, in French in 1958 (see Perelman & Olbrechts-Tyteca, 1958/1969) as *La Nouvelle Rhetorique,* and Toulmin's now classic *The Uses of Argument* (1959) was released by Cambridge University Press the very next year. As it was not until 1969 that the University of Notre Dame Press published John Wilkinson and Purcell Weaver's translation of *The New Rhetoric*, Toulmin's work had a much greater immediate impact on the English speaking philosophical community. One further progenitor of the modern area who also had a marked influence in Europe, but only recently in the United States and Canada, is Arne Naess. His work was first produced in English in 1953 and is an important though often neglected contribution. These scholars are examined in turn with the emphasis placed on their particular contributions to the nature of Argumentation Theory, rather than their complete philosophical outlooks.

Perelman's approach to argumentation rests on several key assumptions. The first is that the separation of argument into different categories, depending on whether it is classed as logic, dialectic or rhetoric, is unfounded. There simply is

---

[1]The philosophical study of argumentation continued through the Middle Ages with refinements and vast alterations and emendations, disputes and rifts. This has been well researched and documented by scholars such as Guthrie (1971), Hamblin (1970), Rescher (1967), Kneale and Kneale (1962), Bochenski (1970), and a host of others. As the focus of this chapter is on the particular turning of the field to Argumentation Theory, I will leave the earlier history in these demonstrably capable hands.

no way, outside of the mathematical sciences and formal logic, to use self-evident premisses in conjunction with logically guaranteed reasoning to secure conclusions. This follows from the denial in *The New Rhetoric* of the existence of the required self-evident starting points: "We do not believe in definitive, unalterable revelations, whatever their nature or origin. And we exclude from our philosophic arsenal all immediate, absolute data, be they termed sensations, rational self-evidence, or mystical intuitions" (1969, p. 510). So, first, every starting point in an argument *can be* challenged, and, therefore, the self-evident input required by the logical truth generating machine cannot get started. Secondly, all arguments based on purely formal models of argument (i.e., formal logic) are, at best, attempts to reduce and translate natural, inherently ambiguous language into formal terms. Such arguments are termed 'quasi-logical' as opposed to logical since there may always be debate concerning their proper form.

The single most significant feature of the program is the idea that the truth is not manifest. That is, there is no way we can point, in the course of an argument, to the truth itself: there is no "natural light" that shines forth from true statements and is lacking in false ones. Argument, therefore, is the only way we have of reaching non-formal truth in the first instance, and so truth itself cannot in turn be appealed to as a criterion for determining which arguments are best. The contrary view, the "Natural Light Theory" holds that when two views are pitted against each other, the true one will, *by virtue of its truth* come out the better. Perelman and Olbrechts-Tyteca explicitly reject such a view, and do not believe that convincing or persuading an audience in the course of an argument means that the view adopted must be the true one. Indeed, the very title of Perelman and Olbrechts-Tyteca's work calls for a re-interpretation of the relationship between truth and rhetoric, i.e., argument. The kind of rhetoric under discussion is "new": it does not emphasize myriad ways in which a speech can be made flowery, but focuses instead on the ways in which the adherence of a particular audience may be increased through reason and argument.

The abandonment of identifiably veridical theses as the goal of argumentation explains why the notion of 'adherence' is so central to Perelman's work. He says in (the very accessible) *The Realm of Rhetoric*, that the purpose of argumentation is " ... to elicit or increase the adherence of the members of an audience to theses that are presented for their consent" (1982, p. 9). After all, if there are no self-evident truths we can only believe propositions more or less, and, when arguing, the arguer's goal will be to increase the audience's *adherence* to the particular proposition or position in question. The adherence should be sufficiently strong to warrant action as well as simple belief. Moreover, the concepts of 'adherence' and 'audience' go hand in hand. One does not argue in isolation. Arguments are about real things being presented to real people: "For argumentation to exist an effective community of minds must be realized at a given moment" (Perelman & Olbrechts-Tyteca, 1958/1969, p. 15). That community is constructed by the speaker, and it is the adherence of that audience that the speaker seeks. Each audience has its accepted beliefs and will honor certain modes of proof and argument: "For since argumentation aims at securing the adherence of those to whom it is addressed, it is, in its entirety, relative to the audience to be influenced" (1969, p. 19). Thus, a persuasive argument aimed at two separate audiences with regard to the same theses might be constructed and presented in entirely different ways. It is the audience that provides one with the initial agreed upon presumptions required to begin the argument, as well as providing the frame for the substance and style of the argumentation.

Not all audiences are created equal; some are elite whereas some are common. Above them all is the *universal audience,* a construct that represents the widest and most discerning audience to which one might address an argument. Philosophy, science, and the "best" arguments generally have the universal audience as the constructed audience: "Everyone constitutes the universal audience from what he knows of his fellow men, in such a way as to transcend the few oppositions he is aware of. Each individual, each culture, has thus its own conception of the universal audience" (Perelman & Olbrechts-Tyteca, 1958/1969, p. 33). And yet, the concept still maintains its force as a result of its construction. The individual arguer must construe her or his arguments as being acceptable to the widest possible group. This means that (barring bald self-deception) the psychological necessity of admitting objections from various audience members, actual or hypothetical, will act as a control on the nature of the argumentation, provided only that the arguer aims it at the universal audience.

Perelman and Olbrechts-Tyteca provide a thorough and useful taxonomy of arguments as used in practical discourse. Their emphasis is heavily on speeches addressed to an audience, and does not focus on dialogic argument as does more recent work. It is surprising that, as important as audience is to Perelman, he pays relatively little attention to dialogic argumentation. There is some mention made of it, but it is not at the core of the book except as an instance of one type of audience. Indeed, dialogic argumentation turns out to be an encounter that must mimic one with a larger audience: "The philosophic significance of the interlocutor's adherence in dialogue is that the interlocutor is regarded as an incarnation of the universal audience" (Perelman & Olbrechts-Tyteca, 1958/1969, p. 37). Perelman and Olbrechts-Tyteca acknowledge that pure "discussion," which is heuristic, as opposed to "debate," which is eristic, are extreme ends on a continuum. Most dialogues fall between the extremes and involve some aspects of both. But, in the end, dialogic argumentation is secondary and derivative to discourse before a larger audience.

Perelman's work raised the flag of argumentation as that which we use to locate the truth, and waved it before the forces of formal logicians and classical rhetoricians. The former group had to begin to confront the truth that formalized argument was radically divorced from actual argumentation, and the latter had to begin the modernization away from the analysis of classical speeches and toward the "new" rhetoric that involved persuasion, adherence, and real audiences. By denying the separabilty of logic and rhetoric Perelman forced argumentation theorists to think along new, integrated lines.

One effect of *The New Rhetoric* and later works by Perelman alone was to emphasize the aridity and irrelevance of formal deductive logic to argumentation. In addition, the abandonment of non-mathematical absolute truth (or, at the very least, our ability to recognize it), the importance of the actual audience being addressed, and the notion of increased adherence as the goal of argumentation all aided in refocusing modern rhetorical studies. Perelman's initial impact, however, was more in communication and rhetorical studies than in philosophy, especially in North America. Although he was certainly not unknown in philosophical circles (see Natanson & Johnstone, 1965), his work has only relatively recently come to the attention of many philosophy-based argumentation scholars.

Toulmin and the DWC Model

A lack of attention was certainly not the problem with the second of the ancestors. Stephen Toulmin's (1969) book, *The Uses of Argument*, has received attention from philosophers, rhetoricians, and communication theorists. The book shares many prejudices with *The New Republic*, most notably the importance of audience ('fields' for Toulmin) and the belief in the irrelevance of formal logic to ordinary discourse. Indeed, a great deal of Toulmin's book is a direct attack on the relevance of formal logic to anything aside from pure mathematics. Writing very much in the "ordinary language" tradition, Toulmin aimed to deflate the claims of those who saw formal logic as the proper arbiter of argumentative correctness.[2] This entailed clarification of several different key concepts.

One such key notion Toulmin introduced was the idea of a 'field' as a domain-relevant arena of discourse. Formal logic, he argued, saw itself as providing criteria for sound argument for every field regardless of its subject matter. This led to the conclusion that only argumentation in formal disciplines could be correct since they alone had sufficient precision and breadth across fields (Toulmin, 1969, p. 43). But if one examines the terminology it becomes clear that much of it is being coopted by logic from ordinary language. Terms like 'possible,' 'necessary,' and 'logical' all have different significance in different areas. The term 'logical' used in an argument about modus ponens would likely require a formal interpretation, while the same word used in a prediction about the Toronto Blue Jays baseball team 1995 pitching rotation would mean something substantially less rigorous than "logically necessary." Toulmin concluded that we could separate aspects of what goes on in argument into those that were *field dependent* and those that were *field invariant*. The new logician, concerned about real argument, would focus on the field invariant aspects that applied across the board (Toulmin, 1969, p. 15). Every argument, for example, is expected to have a claim or conclusion that is put forward as true, while, on the other hand, the sorts of evidence relevant in one field may be irrelevant in another.

The connection between Toulmin's fields and Perelman's audiences has to do with the importance of recognizing variability as a legitimate component in

---

[2]It is not clear who Toulmin had in mind as defender of this position. Unlike his arguments against Kneale and Carnap's respective views on probability, the arguments against the virulent logicism he attacked are not assigned to specific philosophers. In fact, it might be hard to find anyone at the time who held the view he described.

argument analysis. The kinds of data offered, the degree of support it provides, and the level of support required for acceptance of a claim will not be the same in every arena of endeavor. Mathematicians, for example, might require certainty, and settle for nothing less than a full blown *reductio* before abandoning a proposition or accepting its negate. The purchaser of an automobile, on the other hand, may include all sorts of evidence of wildly varying degrees of confirmability, including respected magazine reports, friendly hearsay, and emotional reactions. In short, Toulmin agreed with Perelman that *situation* is relevant to the judgment of an argument: Where is it taking place? What is its subject matter? Who is having the argument? Still, the degree to which situation was relevant was limited, and the search was still focused on finding the field invariant features that could be applied and studied across the board, albeit, in natural settings.

Toulmin's most enduring contribution, of course, was his model of argument. This model, often referred to as the DWC model, purports to provide a geometric representation of actual argumentation as it may occur in a particular situation. An argument normally begins with an assertion, called the *Claim* [C], along with its *Data* [D]. If there is a query, then this usually enthymematic combination will be fleshed out by the *Warrant* [W]. The claim might be something like, "Watch out when you argue with Jack, he'll be a good arguer," along with data such as, "because Jack is a philosophy major." The warrant for inferring this claim from that data might be, "Generally, philosophy majors are good arguers." One can also add a *Qualifier* [Q], such as, "so, probably, Jack will be … ," and/or a *Rebuttal* [R], such as, "unless Jack is a failing student." Finally, there is the *Backing* [B] of the warrant that appeals to generally held theories and presumptions held by subscribers to the field. A possible backing for the current example might be, "Philosophy majors usually study argument and become adept through writing and thinking critically." All put together, the model looks like Fig. 1.1.

This model is a far cry from the standard Gentzen-style Natural Deduction layout of an argument. First of all, it includes items actually found in arguments, and pays attention to the process of justifying and defending an assertion, rather than itemizing a formal justification according to a set of transformation rules. One will note that there is still a distinctly deductive feel to Toulmin's model. The data seems to be a minor premiss and the warrant the major premiss. We can also insert a modal qualifier, and likely even formalize the rebuttal. Still, the fact that this can be done does not mean that the model is essentially deductive, just that different models can

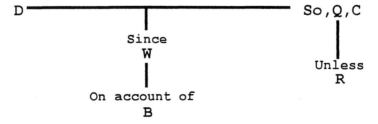

FIG. 1.1.   Toulmin's DWC Model

intertranslate. The importance from the point of view of Argumentation Theory is that the move is away from modeling after mathematical thought and toward the jurisprudential. In both cases, the support and justification are important, but in the latter they are also available to the arguer.

It is also important to note that the DWC model assumes that arguments generally take place *between people.* The warrant, backing, and rebuttal all come into play as required. That is, the argument is presented in a bare way and the remainder is added when an interlocutor demands further information. This was one of the first instances of the awareness of the essentially dialogic nature of argumentation, albeit in a limited way. The presence of the interlocutor is hinted at rather than asserted in Toulmin. We must assume that the warrant, backing and rebuttal are in response to something; and what could that be aside from a request from a person for further information? So the argument is still laid out with one speaker in mind insofar as the result is what is produced by one person with the prompting of an invisible partner. Still, Toulmin did recognize that arguments are often interactive and that what happens in them is frequently a function of that interaction.

Toulmin's greatest weakness, from one point of view, lies in the inherently adversarial nature of his approach. "Logic (we may say) is generalized jurisprudence" (1969, p. 7). In other words, what we do is an unrefined version of what goes on in a courtroom. Primarily this means it is adversarial and zero-sum. There will be one winner and one loser, and each argument will be judged and assessed independently. As good a start as Toulmin's model was, it conceived of argument as an intellectual contest as opposed to an episode between two persons centering on dissensus.

Naess' Precization

Arne Naess, the Norwegian philosopher and logician, is the third grandsire of contemporary Argumentation Theory. His greatest influence has been on European, and particularly German and Dutch, theorizing. Naess, unlike Toulmin and Perelman, began by thinking and working in dialectical terms. Argument for him was something that happened between people in an interactive context. In addition, the development of the first stages of dialogue theory or formal dialectic are attributable to him in *Interpretation and Preciseness* (1953), almost 20 years prior to Hamblin's introduction of dialogue games in 1970. Naess developed rules for governing interactions that put dialectic at center stage. Van Eemeren, Grootendorst, and Kruiger (1987) quote from his *Wie fordert man heute die empirische Bewegung?* (1956):

> Perhaps the best word to describe what I mean is 'dialectic.' ... In my terminology, debate, or dialectic, is a part of the investigation; that is to say, it is a form of systematic intersubjective verbal communication whereby misunderstandings can be cleared up and individual points of view can be submitted for approval or rejection. This is not meant as a normative definition, but as an approximation to a descriptive definition.. (p. 115).

Naess (1966) specifically saw language as being context dependent. A set of words having a particular meaning on one occasion, he says, might be *"expressing something quite different in another context"* (p. 9; emph. orig.). And, again,

> [S]poken and written expression are not abstracted from the context of individuals' speaking, writing, listening to and reading these expressions ... The basic materials for us are occurrences of utterances. Thus, "It rains" is in itself no immediate object of our concern, but we are concerned with "it rains" as uttered or heard, or instances of that sentence in texts. (Naess, 1953, p. 1)

Words only have meaning as used by people in a particular context. Consequently, what becomes crucial is understanding the terminology used in a given situation: the meanings as communicated between the users of language. With this in mind, Naess focuses on the notion of *precization*, a technique for creating finer and finer linguistic agreements among protagonists. Naess is concerned to find a method for making expressions more and more precise in order that participants in a dialogue move closer to understanding and resolution. Of two expressions *a* and *b*, one will normally be more precise than the other if they share a set of alternative expressions but *a* has fewer alternatives than *b*. Naess (1953) defines *a* as more precise than *b* under the following circumstances.

> If, and only if, every synonymic alternative to *a* is also a synonymic alternative to *b*, and there is at least one synonymic alternative to *b* which is not a synonymic alternative to *a*, and *a* admits of at least one synonymic alternative, then *a* will be said to be *more precise* than *b*. (p.6)

This is stated less technically of expressions *U* and *T* in *Communication and Argument* (Naess, 1966):

> That an expression *U* is a *precization* of an expression *T* means here that all reasonable interpretations of *U* are reasonable interpretations of *T*, and that there is at least one reasonable interpretation of *T* which is *not* a reasonable interpretation of *U*. (p. 39)

Once having established the basic notion, Naess goes on to provide rules and guidelines for precizating expressions in the course of an argument. This requires extensive clarifications of modes of definition, and allows, in the far more technical 1953 work, a formalization of the concept of precization and its relation to various modes of definition. The impact of this work is seen most clearly in that of Barth and Krabbe, as well as van Eemeren and Grootendorst. It should be noted that there seems to be an implicit assumption in Naess' work that precision leads to or means understanding, but that is not explicitly argued. Indeed, one might claim that a certain amount of ambiguity can be important in argument insofar as it permits a greater focus on the main issues and avoids overly detailed exposition. Naess, however, fears "pseudo agreement" wherein two arguers think they are in agreement but really are not, more than the continuation of lengthy argumentation. Avoidance of this pitfall is the virtue of the axiom that by being precise one promotes understanding and focus on the issues.

Dialecticians

The three authors presented so far have all been instrumental in moving the focus of Argumentation Theory from the argument as artifact to the argument as human process. Their work had great impact, albeit in generally distinct arenas. Both Perelman and Toulmin were (and are) widely referenced by researchers in Communication Theory and Speech Theory, but Perelman has not received a great deal of attention from philosophers. Naess has mostly been attended to by Europeans and, like the rest of the formalists, largely ignored by Communication Theory.

At the time that Toulmin and Perelman were writing, Informal Logicians were teaching students Critical Reasoning and fallacies primarily through texts like Copi's *Introduction to Logic* (1961). In this style, fallacies are presented in a brief fashion using examples that were mostly invented or taken out of context. It was not until 1971 that Howard Kahane, responding to the changing times and the demands of the students of the 1960s, published *Logic and Contemporary Rhetoric: The Use of Reason in Everyday Life*. The "radical change" was that Kahane's book took current examples from newspapers and periodicals dealing with issues students cared about or, at least, recognized. This meant that the fallacies were more *situated* than in older books. It was still the case, however, that philosophers concerned with Argumentation Theory were exclusively involved in Informal Logic, and primarily concerned with pedagogy. It was the study of fallacies and the pedagogic demands of Critical Reasoning courses that directed their work and concerns. There were notable exceptions to this, namely, the Australian philosopher C.L. Hamblin, and American philosophers Henry Johnstone and Nicholas Rescher. While all three had different approaches, their outlooks were connected by the clear vision they had of a need for change in the then current approach.

In Hamblin's now classic work *Fallacies* (1970), he argued that the traditional approach, "the standard treatment," of fallacies did not work. Instead, if we are to understand fallacies we must first understand argument: "Someone who merely makes false statements, however absurd, is innocent of fallacy unless the statements constitute or express an argument" (p. 224). Hamblin's discussion of 'argument,' echoing Perelman, allows that the concept is not nearly as neat as logicians, both formal and informal, would like to make out, but is, rather, dependent on the context: "The actual logical relation between premises and conclusion may be anything at all" (p. 230). Fallacy, for Hamblin, is also a question of context. He insisted that fallacies and errors in argumentation really only made sense in the context of the dynamics of dialectic. Of the fallacy of equivocation, for example, he says, that "we almost never suppose any word to be equivocal until we get into trouble with it" (p. 294). This is as against the Standard Treatment where fallacies are taken to be identifiable occurrences that can be found in individual arguments.

In his penultimate chapter, "Formal Dialectic," Hamblin acknowledges the vital importance of argument as something that occurs *between people*. He introduces, in light of that insight, a method of formal dialectic or set of dialogue games. These are among the first attempts to create a system of move–counter-move that would keep track of arguments and assumptions used by disputers. The central idea is that in argument each arguer acquires certain "commitments" that are figuratively placed in one's "commitment-store." The object of the game is to force one's partner into committing to inconsistent assertions. This formalization allowed for the investigation of such crucial notions as burden of proof, inconsistency, and winning in the context of argument.

Henry Johnstone Jr. was among the first North Americans to write about argumentation. Like most philosophers working in the area, he was strongly among the dialecticians, the argumentation theorists who see a specific and special mode of argumentation with its own set of values, attitudes and procedures that can be labeled 'dialectic.' To do dialectic is to search for a result that is indisputable either because it is the truth or because it stands up better than any of its competitors to opposing views. One does not have to believe that dialectics produces the truth, merely that the truth can stand up to fair argumentation.[3] A *dialectician* believes that argument should be conducted according to rules and conventions that serve to identify the theory or view that best withstands attack and criticism. A *rhetorician*, on the other hand, believes that such rules and procedures are themselves objects of rhetorical procedure and, so, part and parcel of the theory it sets out to defend (see, Weimer, 1984). Aside from Johnstone, other dialectical philosophers include Rescher and Toulmin, whereas the rhetoricians mentioned so far include Perelman and Naess.

Johnstone is an extreme dialectician. He believed quite strongly that there are distinct modes of argumentation that are dependent upon an arguer's intent. In particular, philosophical argumentation, (along with other forms such as scientific,) is special insofar as it has as its goal the idea of truth or, at least, the clarity of a vision, or the investigation of a theory according to rules and principles of rationality. In his criticisms of Perelman and Olbrechts-Tyteca, Johnstone is particularly concerned with their inability or neglect in distinguishing between philosophical dialectic on the one hand, and rhetoric or ordinary argument on the other. In the latter instance, but not the former, *persuading* one's opposer is the key focus: "The philosopher's aim in arguing has usually been more than merely to secure adherence to his thesis. More specifically, no conscientious philosopher would be satisfied by assent brought about by methods concealed from his audience" (1978, p. 133).

Rhetoric for Johnstone, even Perelman and Olbrechts-Tyteca's "new rhetoric," is not appropriate for the dialectical investigation of philosophical issues. When pursuing philosophical truth, one does not use rhetorical techniques. One follows fair and correct argumentation practices designed to lead to the discovery of the most rational and logical view. As a result of this, Johnstone is a good representative of one who holds that the persuade–convince dichotomy discussed above is an important and viable distinction. He does not, however, directly confront Perelman's arguments against the position that we are incapable of distinguishing

---

[3]One not need be a realist about truth to be a dialectician. It suffices to hold the view that the best theory is the one that holds up best to specific kinds of scrutiny, namely, dialectic.

between the rhetorical and the dialectical on any systematic basis. This means he never deals with questions of the following sort: Is an emphatic tone of voice enough to make an argument rhetorical? Is the presentation of a chain of similar but cleverly related arguments sufficient? What about the anticipation of counter-arguments? Is it rhetorical if one builds in avenues of response or escape? Aren't the decisions an author makes regarding what becomes body text and what becomes footnotes rhetorical decisions?[4]

Also a staunch dialectician, Rescher's work in the area of Argumentation Theory goes back well before such a field existed. Although he may, perhaps, never have seen himself as a participant in this specific field, a great deal of his efforts have been directed toward the clarification of concepts crucial to the area. As his work is generally well known to those in the philosophical community, it suffices to point out that his examination of the notions of presumption, burden of proof, and dialectics provide excellent examples of the dialectical or critical rationalist approach to Argumentation Theory.[5] The true role of argumentation, according to Rescher, is to lead us to well founded beliefs by following the accepted rules of rationality. Argument often is adversarial and has as its goal the moving of one person in a dispute from one point of view to another. But dialectics, while it may be adversarial, can move to 'inquiry,' where, when dealing with a thesis, one has "... the aim of refining its formulation, uncovering its basis of rational support, and assessing its relative weight" (1977, p. 47). This is done first in unilateral inquiry where, presumably the goal is not to win insofar as one is arguing with oneself. Consequently, the object must be to determine the best course of action. We can then apply this conception in turn to a dyadic context wherein the aim is investigating the probative status of a proposition or theory.

Grice and the Cooperative Principle

One philosopher who almost certainly did not consider himself involved in Argumentation Theory but became very important, especially to its European and Communication Theoretic branches, is the British philosopher Paul Grice. His 1975 essay, "Logic & Conversation" (1975/1989), has had a major impact. Grice's main point is that normal conversation is a cooperative enterprise between a speaker and a listener that follows intricate written and implicit rules. The main rule followed, he claimed, is the Cooperative Principle [CP]: "Make your conversational contribution such as is required, at the stage at which it occurs by the accepted purpose or direction of the talk exchange in which you are engaged" (Grice, 1975/1989, p.

---

[4]See Weimer's "Why All Knowing Is Rhetorical" (1984) for an interesting discussion of this from the perspective of Argumentation Theory.

[5]An excellent overview of Rescher's thinking can be found in a special issue of the journal, *Informal Logic* (1992, *14:1*), which was dedicated to his work. His most central book in this area is, in my opinion, *Dialectics* (1977). There Rescher defends the rules of rationality against scepticism as well as putting forward rules for the conduct of rational inquiry.

26). In other words, one is expected to follow the usual or normal routines of conversation. A contribution to a conversation must not be, and, as a matter of fact, is not, random, but instead follows as a result of the existing conversation and the normal rules and procedures we follow. This overarching principle, the CP, is further articulated by Grice as four maxims that govern the quantity of conversation, the quality of what is said (i.e., truth), its relevance and manner (i.e., perspicacity).

One problem is that Grice's rules seem to be derived from a relatively narrow cultural tradition. In some cultures, for example, saying only the minimum is both the exception and a sign of potentially rude taciturnity. In others, the exact opposite is true. Consequently, due to these and other considerations, certain fallacies such as emotive language, equivocation, *ad hominem*, and *ad misericordiam* (to mention a few) might be applied according to totally different precepts. One of Grice's (1975/1989) basic rules, for example, is the rule of Quality which states: "*Super-maxin*: Try to make your contribution one that is true" (p. 27). That is, one ought always tell the truth. But in many cultures (including, arguably, his own) this rule simply does not apply in many situations. Insulting one's host by not praising the food, drink, or accommodations is often considered a far greater fault than equivocating or, even, outright lying (see Bavelas, et al., 1990).

The rules Grice presented are not intended as rules he invented in order for conversations to proceed smoothly. Rather, they are rules one discovers in examining the way conversations actually proceed. Consequently, one response to the cultural variations that will inevitably be found is that each culture will have a maxim concerning, for example, quantity, but the understanding of how those maxims are fulfilled may well vary.

The most crucial insight Grice offered covered what happens when a maxim is violated, that is, what do we do when the Cooperative Principle is not followed? While a violation can occur for various reasons, it is when the maxim is "flouted" that is most significant to argumentation. In this case it is apparent to the listener that the speaker, in uttering statement p is in violation of the Cooperative Principle if the statement p is taken at face value. For Grice, this means that the statement could not, *ipso facto*, be so taken, and the hearer has to look for and locate an alternative meaning to the words or symbolism for the expression. In other words, the assumption is that the person with whom one is communicating is making sense and is following the normal rules of ordinary conversation. In such a situation we say that the speaker has performed a *conversational implicature*. Grice (1975/1989) described this as follows:

> One who says p will be said to have implicated q when,
>
> 1. He is observing the maxims or, at least, the CP;
>
> 2. supposing he intends q is required to make his saying p consistent with assumption 1;
>
> 3. the speaker assumes the listener will infer q from p because of 2. (p. 30)

So, one will be said to be making a conversational implicature when one is observing the CP, and the implicatum is needed for an average listener to make sense of the speaker's remarks. This covers, for example, many colloquialisms such as, "He's between a rock and a hard place." It also covers remarks and answers requiring inside information, such as someone inquiring if the always late rising Thomas has arrived yet, and receiving the answer, "Has the sun set?" By strict rules, this is an irrelevant response, but since we (a) assume the speaker is following the CP, we (b) assume that what was said is relevant, so we (c) infer that what she really means is that Thomas will not be here because it is too early. Moreover, we further assume that the speaker knows or assumes we will get the point of the remark and not be misled.

Grice's CP and its correlate conversational implicature provided a handy framework for simply explicating the communicative axiom that *communicators work together to provide meaning to messages*. It explained neatly why we still understand each other even though messages are often incomplete and must be fleshed out by having the recipient add missing ingredients. When the missing component is a premiss, then we say the communication was enthymematic. When the message needs to be reconsidered in order to make sense, we say it must be a conversational implicature. Especially attractive to Communication Theory and seminal in recent work in Argumentation Theory are the basic notions that 1] the recipient of a message is an active partner in the conversation, and 2] that apparent violations of the Cooperative Principle indicate *not* that a communicator has done something wrong, but that the message cannot be taken literally. Most generally, Grice gave a gloss to the universally held view within Communication Theory that a sender's messages are routinely incomplete and must be filled in or fleshed out by the recipient.

The Speech Theorists

At the same time the philosophers just discussed were writing, changes were also taking place among scholars in Communication Theory who concentrated on argumentation. One vantage point for observing the metamorphosis was the *Journal of the American Forensic Association* [JAFA]. This journal was the organ of the American Forensic Association, dedicated to the advancement and organization of formal debating. Members were primarily college, junior college, and high school debating coaches, and the journal carried news of the U.S. National Debate Tournament and featured articles devoted to debating technique. Over a span of 20 years, the journal was to evolve beyond its original purpose to a platform for scholars concerned with the communicative and philosophical aspects of interactional argumentation. Following the evolution of JAFA, now renamed *Argumentation and Advocacy*, is to witness the creation and substantiation of a new discipline.

The first real sign occurred in 1970, when an article entitled, "The Limits of Logic" by G. D. Mortenson and R. L. Anderson argued that formal logic was inadequate for the comprehension and representation of everyday or marketplace argument. Subsequently, in 1975, Wayne Brockriede published "Where is Argument?", and in 1977, D. J. O'Keefe published "Two Concepts of Argument." In the former article, Brockriede claimed that argument is not something that is merely found in editorials and texts, but rather is a dynamic process occurring between people that has identifiable characteristics and may be found virtually anywhere. An argument for Brockriede has to be inferential without being an entailment, provide reasons for a choice among competing claims, and involve uncertainty as to outcome. He also requires that the argument take place within a frame of reference the participants share, and that the arguers expose themselves to the authentic risk of belief change. Two years later, D. J. O'Keefe introduced a distinction that became crucial for future writers. He distinguished between argument$_1$ and argument$_2$, where the former denotes an abstract or concrete object that is the result of an individual's *making an argument*, whereas the latter designates that process in which two arguers are engaged when *having an argument*.

Wenzel offered several further distinctions when, in 1980, he allowed for three separate perspectives on argument. The first, the traditional category of argument as object, e.g., a syllogism, he termed 'product.' The second, 'procedure,' encompassed the rhetorical skills and insights accumulated over the ages. From the point of view of procedure, argument is something that can be analyzed for its persuasive impact and its use of rhetorical technique. 'Process' was the term that described what is often called 'dialectic': two individuals using critical rationality to investigate or determine the truth. Many of the problems plaguing Argumentation Theory, he claimed, were a result of attempting to find one all encompassing approach for three distinct endeavors.

What was most significant about these writings was their integration of logical and argumentation concepts that went beyond the traditional categories in Communication Theory. They witnessed an awareness of a growth toward the investigation of dialogic argumentation while at the same time holding onto the basal concepts of rhetorical and speech studies. It was, after all, not only philosophy that had concentrated on the static argument, but rhetoric as well. Concern with the analysis of public speeches was to be replaced by a focus on the interaction undertaken by people in disagreement. This required new concepts and distinctions, such as argument$_1$ and argument$_2$, that would permit the scholar to differentiate between different concerns.

One major influence on Argumentation Theory and, indeed, Communication Theory in general has been the Social Constructvitist approach. Willard, in a 1978 article entitled, "A Reformulation of the Concept of Argument: The Constructivist/Interactionist Foundations of a Sociology of Argument," utilizes Personal Construct Theory and Chicago School Interactionism to define argument "as a specific kind of social relationship or encounter" (p. 121). More particularly, *"argument is a kind of interaction in which people maintain what they construe to be mutually exclusive propositions"* (p. 125, emph. orig.). This approach, popular in Communication Theory, meant that Argumentation Theory had a descriptive role as well as its traditionally normative function. In order to understand *argument*, we must begin with *arguers*. Arguments, for Willard, only exist as used by people arguing, and, furthermore, when people are arguing, practically anything they do might be an argument.

With the enunciation of this position, there suddenly existed camps of competing theories. The extremes were represented at one end by Willard and his very broad conception of 'argument.' The other (at least as an exemplar) was defended by Burleson (1981) who maintained that conceptions of 'argument' must be suitable for argumentation scholars, that arguments themselves had to be essentially verbal, and definitions should specifically exclude moves and styles that are not worthy of the honorific argument. Because, he maintains, argument is a broadly used and fuzzy concept, a characterization "based on ordinary usage will necessarily be so inclusive as to encompass a wide range of events that have little theoretical meaning as 'arguments'" (p. 969). Argumentation Theory, according to Burleson, has no business studying shouting matches, fights, crying, or squabbling.

The Speech Theorists, as we may call them, come to Argumentation Theory from a different perspective than the Informal Logicians. They begin with the arguer as someone who is confronting the task of persuasion (a term which for them is not derogatory.) Much more involved with the rhetorical tradition, Speech Theorists need the speech to be associated with the speaker for it to have meaning or be liable to analysis. The Informal Logician has historically focused on the argument as an artifact, a thing that can be analyzed for validity, fallaciousness and adequacy independently of the context of its use. In speech act terms, one can say that while the philosophers are focused on the locutionary act, the debaters are more interested in the illocutionary act and how the argument is created and used. It thus becomes important for them to be able to define argument in a way broad enough to allow its use in many natural situations, but narrow enough to maintain some constancy of meaning.

The Amsterdam School

While American scholars were debating the scope and meaning of the term 'argument,' in Holland more formal approaches to interactive argument were being developed. The first of these approaches was pioneered by Frans van Eemeren and Rob Grootendorst at the University of Amsterdam. Called *Pragma-Dialectics*, the approach relies on the actual practices and assertions of arguers in a situated argumentation, and focuses on two or more persons arguing as opposed to an argument as an artifact. Thus their approach is *pragmatic* because they are concerned with the practical task of arguing, and *dialectic* because they see argument as a social process occurring between two arguers. The Pragma-Dialectic school derives from the branch of Communication Theory known as Discourse Analysis, and draws very heavily on Austin's (1975) and especially Searle's (1969) notion of speech acts. Arguments, for the Dutch School, are meant to justify a standpoint to the satisfaction of a rational judge, similar to Perelman and Olbrecht-Tyteca's (1958/1969) "universal audience," according to agreed upon rules.

Since their concern is dialectics, the speech acts as used by Austin and Searle are insufficiently complex for argumentation which requires interaction between individual units. Consequently, van Eemeren and Grootendorst (1984) introduced the notion of an *illocutionary act complex*:

> This act complex is composed of elementary illocutions which belong to the category of *assertives* and which at the sentence level maintain a one-to-one ratio with (grammatical) sentences. The total constellation of the elementary illocutions constitutes the illocutionary act complex of *argumentation*, which at a higher level maintains, as a single whole, a one-to-one ratio with a (grammatical) sentence sequence. (p. 34). In other words, an argument is composed of individual speech acts that, taken collectively form a single illocutionary act complex. In order to be successful the illocutionary act must be understood by the listener, (whence the importance of Grice.)

Clearly, however, simply being understood is not enough for most disputers. When transmitting an argument one requires that it be understood, but one also wants the argument to achieve something, that is, *to convince the listener*. For this reason, van Eemeren and Grootendorst, unlike Austin and Searle, place great importance on the *perlocutionary* aspect of the speech act. When one is arguing the effect one wants to have, i.e., convincing, is crucial to understanding the process as one of arguing. Indeed, van Eemeren and Grootendorst are very concerned to distinguish between rational decisions by the listener that are a result of considerations intended by the communicator, and those that are either accidental or intended to achieve other non-rational effects, e.g., arouse the listener's emotions. In argument, "the listener is expected to decide on rational grounds whether or not he should allow the perlocutionary effect desired by the speaker to be brought about" (van Eemeren & Grootendorst, 1984, p. 28).

Extending Searle's analysis to a set of sentences comprising an argumentation, van Eemeren and Grootendorst specify felicity, sincerity, recognition, satisfaction, and other conditions for argumentation both pro and contra. A speech act can, for example, succeed on the illocutionary level as an argumentation by being so understood, but might not succeed on the perlocutionary level by failing to convince. The Pragma-Dialectic approach also provides them with a platform for the analysis of argumentation into processual stages permitting a deeper analysis by allowing for the examination of interactions per exchange. They are also able to provide an analysis of enthymematic arguments (van Eemeren & Grootendorst, 1982, 1983) and fallacies (van Eemeren & Grootendorst, 1987).[6]

The Amsterdam School of van Eemeren and Grootendorst is an attempt to try and model arguing while, at the same time, holding fast to the standards of rationality and orderliness. Not surprisingly, a great deal of what ordinary people might describe as argument must be lost as a result of its being non-rational, insufficiently verbal (and so too ambiguous to identify,) or by dint of its following

---

[6]An interesting overview of their position along with both criticisms and extensions may be found in the journal *Argumentation* (see van Eemeren & Grootendorst, 1989). The issue is dedicated to argumentation and speech act theory.

procedures or styles of argument that vary from the established models. Much argument simply does not follow a sufficiently routinized process to allow the identification of the requisite components for speech act identification (cf., Jacobs, 1989). Indeed, van Eemeren and Grootendorst's description of the process of organizing a naturally located argumentation into one suitable for linguistic analysis involves no fewer than four "dialectical transformations." Instructions for the application of these translation rules are reminiscent of nothing so much as the formalization of ordinary language into formal logic. In the transformation known as "deletion", for example, we are told that elements that are irrelevant include "elaborations, clarifications, anecdotes, and side-lines" (1989, p. 375). It is quite possible, however, that these discarded bits might very well contain the most significant information that would allow the listener to understand the argument. Often, for example, a reiteration, sideline, or example may have more communicative force than the alleged "real" core argument. Consequently, a useful model must be watched carefully lest it carry away in the name of uniformity that naturalness it was specifically trying to identify.

Barth's Formalism

In an avowedly more formal and classically logical vein, one finds E. M. Barth, a major force in the development and propagation of systems of formal dialectic. A student of Arne Naess and E.W. Beth, she is in a tradition traced directly to P. Lorenzen and K. Lorenz, wherein formal dialectic is captured in formal logic. To date this enterprise was most fully articulated in her collaboration with Erik Krabbe, *From Axiom to Dialogue*. There they write,

> Following Lorenzen and Kuno Lorenz, we shall show that the logical constants can be defined, *in various manners*, by rules for their use in *critical dialogues*, and the concepts of *logical truth* and logically *valid argument*, too, in such a manner that the *extensions* of these concepts are exactly those we know from other set-ups ('garbs') of two-valued, or of constructive, or of minimal logic. One obtains *exactly* the same 'logical truths' and *exactly* the same valid arguments as in other descriptions of these three logics. (Barth & Krabbe, 1982, p. 24, emph. orig.)

As this sentiment indicates, the bases of the systems Barth and Krabbe present are deeply rooted in elementary formal logic. To the usual essentials, they add operators that allow for the interactive aspects of the dialectical process. These include asserting one's willingness to defend a claim or querying how an opponent will defend it, and declaring for oneself or pointing out for an opponent a propositional burden.

Conflicts of avowed opinions begin by the discussants agreeing upon a formal system of dialogue rules. They then begin to explore each other's commitment set, inquire as to defenses and other commitments, and aim to resolve the disagreement by showing that one or the other holds an inconsistent set, thereby forcing the abandonment of the disputed statement. Prior to that outcome, the discussion must be carried out according to agreed upon rules of rational behavior. Their rules of dialectic are based upon the classical laws of propostional logic, e.g., if one is committed to $P \supset Q$, and it is shown that one must also be committed to P, then one is, *ipso facto*, committed to Q. Similarly, if one asserts $[P \vee (Q \& R)]$, and it is shown that P is false, then one is committed to $(Q \& R)$. The systems also include rules for behavior that specifically preclude abusive, irrelevant, or otherwise inappropriate argumentative moves. One strong rule available for adoption is such that if it is adopted then, "a debater who is insulted, ridiculed or otherwise abused (fired from his/her job, sent to an asylum or physically hurt) without having committed any non-permitted ... action in the course of the discussion, has won the discussion as a whole" (Barth & Krabbe, 1982, p. 63).

One might wonder just how much solace an arguer committed to an asylum might draw from having crowing rights over a more wicked or powerful opponent. One might also wonder how many arguments really do involve only those moves capable of being mirrored within a propositional calculus. Certainly, some moves made in many arguments will be representable in this way, but many will not. Barth and Krabbe are well aware of this. They see their endeavor as *part* of the Theory of Argumentation, not as the whole story: *"The subject called 'Logic' corresponds to that part of the Theory of Argumentation that studies systems of language-invariant formal3 dialectical rules and language-dependent formal2 dialectical rules based on (formal2) syntactical rules"* (p. 75, emph. orig.). (Where "formal2" indicates the shape of an object, and "formal3" indicates formal in the sense of following specified rules.) So, for them, logic as part of Argumentation Theory is the study of dialectical rules of procedure accepted across languages and dialectical transformation rules inherent in language structure based upon the classical deductive rules of formal logic.

The Informal Logicians

One of the deepest skeins running throughout Argumentation Theory is the tension between the normative and descriptive. Traditionally, argument has been not so much studied as prescribed. What investigations have been made into argument per se have been organized around the desire to increase one's ability to argue rationally. While part and parcel of the study of argument, at the very least, is a modest descriptive component, for traditional Informal Logicians, this might involve nothing more than the identification of premises and conclusions, arguments and subarguments, fallacies, and irrelevancies. One will be instructed to lay out an argument in a certain form, that is, to "describe" or "diagram" the argument in some official standardized way (see, for example, Johnson & Blair, 1983). In other words, comparatively little attention is paid to the way in which people actually *do* conduct arguments as opposed to the way people *ought to* conduct arguments.

Practically every text used in critical reasoning courses has methods for laying out arguments, and in doing so, the analyst selects those components that are crucial to understanding the argument and deselects those considered inessential, misleading, trivial, or redundant. (This is not solely the habit of the Informal Logicians. As mentioned earlier, van Eemeren and Grootendorst followed this same line in the Pragma-Dialectic approach.) Johnson and Blair, for example, tell us that we must "sift through the rhetoric" (1983, p. 80),[7] in order to get through to the actual argument, as if there were some clear delineation between what is "merely rhetorical" and what is "clearly substantial." The assumption crucial to Informal Logic is not just that there is a difference between rhetoric and non-rhetoric, but [1] that the difference is readily identifiable, and [2] that the rhetorical, unlike the non-rhetorical, is not crucial to understanding and/or analyzing an argument.

The bread and butter of the Informal Logician is the fallacy. It may be described as a mistake, or as an argument that looks good and is not, or as a sophistical trap laid out by an unscrupulous arguer, and, indeed, it may be any one of these. Traditionally, (and by that I mean until very recently,) fallacies have been described along with explanations, examples, and/or criteria for their identification (e.g., Fogelin & Sinnott-Armstrong, 1991; Gilbert, 1979, 1996; Johnson & Blair, 1983, 1993). Recently, however, there has been a radical change. The current view is moving more and more to the notion that fallacies, if they are useful at all, can only be really understood in context. That is, any given "fallacy" can only be labeled as such after determining that the specific situation in which it is used is improper. Although its roots are in Hamblin (1970), this was more recently propounded by Walton (1989) who wrote that judgments about fallacies "need to be backed up by evidence from the given, particular text of discourse of the argument being put under scrutiny" (p. 170). This view, though by no means universally accepted, (it would be opposed by Govier, 1987, and Johnson & Blair, 1987) is compelling. This is especially so because one can almost always provide examples of arguments that meet the criteria for a specific fallacy, but that nonetheless seem to be good arguments. Walton cites the *argumentum ad verecundiam* (appeal to authority) as a fallacy that is often not fallacious; we are forever in need of experts, and the issue is *how* one uses them rather than *that* one uses them. Threats, to cite another example, are instances of the *argumentum ad baculum*, or appeal to force. But, if a female employee threatens her supervisor with sexual harassment charges if he does not stop his unsuitable remarks, is a fallacy committed? One would think not. Consequently, the directive, "do not commit fallacies," must be altered or, at least, explicated to mean that one ought not perform certain argumentative moves in certain situations.

The essential change to Argumentation Theory from the point of view of Informal Logic is the emphasis on situation. The impact is great because the field is so heavily prescriptive. The more prescriptive an endeavor, the more important

---

[7]This phrase has been removed from the third edition of *Logical Self-Defense* (Johnson & Blair, 1993). This deletion is indicative of the trend even within Informal Logic toward the importance of more contextual and situated argument.

that it be able to produce general rules of conduct. If Informal Logic can only determine such rules by examining each individual situation, then its generality and ability to provide guides to argumentation behavior is limited. The changes down the road that will be forthcoming in Informal Logic as a result of this new emphasis on situation will be dramatic as the outlook must alter from one of identifying allegedly regular patterns to one of inspecting particular situations for contextual clues. As contact between the divergent groups becomes greater, the pressure on Informal Logic to deal with more real argumentative situations increases (witness for example, Walton, 1992). Simply put, the ideal must, and will, come closer to the real if the field is to maintain its significance within the general realm of Argumentation Theory.

Communication Theorists

The focus on particularity, while somewhat foreign to philosophy, is inherent in that part of Discourse Analysis focusing on conversational interaction. This field, a subarea of Communication Theory, studies actual conversations in order to determine the rules and procedures being followed by the participants. With respect to argumentation, the basal assumption is articulated by Jacobs and Jackson (1982): "The presence of argument signals potential or actual troubles in conversation while its absence indicates the presence of a 'working agreement' in conversation" (p. 206). For Discourse Analysis, the presence of an argument means that something has gone wrong and requires repair. The basis is that each non-phatic utterance in a conversation, (*say a request*) can be met with a preferred, (*request is granted*) or dis-preferred, (*request is denied*) response. If the dis-preferred response occurs, then the conversation must cope with that disruption while, at the same time, maintaining sufficient equilibrium for conversation to proceed.

The Discourse Analysis approach sees argument not only as situation specific, but also as utilizing rules and procedures that are a function of that situation as well as the nature and precise relationships and personalities *of the participants*. This applies to such basic notions as proof and acceptability: "recipients and authors of arguable turns jointly work out the amount and kind of support required to get agreement" (Jacobs & Jackson, 1980, p. 262). This throws, for example, an interesting light on enthymemes. To what degree an enthymeme must be explicated will be a function of the arguers, their agreement and/or disagreement. A skeptical conversational partner will demand a fuller explication than an accepting partner or one who is a disagreement avoider. So, while the Informal Logicians use "good argument" to indicate that process of critical rationality that applies across the board to all (most) arguments in all (most) situations, Discourse Analysts see agreement as an operational convenience in a social context. Each perspective provides distinct conclusions for what is good and bad argumentation.

With regard to the importance of individual differences, B. O'Keefe (1988) has done very interesting work that is relevant to argumentation, especially when trying to determine possible causes for its success and failure. She describes three different types of *message design logic* (MDL). Each design logic determines how an individual constructs (and very likely interprets) communicative messages. The first logic, known as the *expressive message design* logic, is quite literal. The purpose of communication, from the point of view of this MDL, is to express one's thoughts and answers and impart them to one's partner. The expressive recipient assumes that messages are intended to be taken at face value and does so. The second MDL is the *conventional*. A conventional communicator understands that conversation, argument, and communication in general are governed by social rules, and, in communicating, one is, as it were, playing a game. For the conventional MDL, some things may not be said, or, at least, may not be said directly depending on the social conventions governing the particular situation. The most sophisticated MDL is the *rhetorical*. The rhetorical communicator sees not just that there are rules governing communicative interaction, but that assuming different roles or personae itself results in the creation and utililization of different rules. Consequently, the rhetorical message design logic may create situations through the adoption of rhetorical roles and patterns best suited to a given context.

The implications for Argumentation Theory are complex. To begin with, it would seem that the ideal put forward as the best arguer from the point of view of classical Informal Logic, on B. O'Keefe's model, would be an expressive message design logic. After all, practically every critical thinking text explains how everything but the core message must be eliminated from the argument before it is suitable for analysis. So, given the rule-delimited nature of argumentation as conceived by Informal Logic, it may be that the conventional MDL is the most appropriate choice for "best." It is, however, very interesting (if not ironic) that the most subtle, attentive, and flexible communicators, the rhetorical MDL users, would most certainly not be the group Informal Logic would identify as the best arguers. This last group relies far too much on the particular situation and context and too little on the argument *qua argument*.

Another question arises if we try to think of the establishment of rules across message design logics. Perhaps the way in which one communicates is relevant to the rules one ought follow in so doing. Finally, various mistakes, fallacies, and errors, might be so construed simply because the observer utilizes a message design logic different from the participant[s], resulting in (perhaps) a negative assessment of a form of argument alien to the observer.

Another area of Communication Theory research relevant to Argumentation Theory, (of which more will be said in chapter 5) includes work on goals as components of all communicative and especially argumentative episodes. It is taken for granted in the area of goals research that all communicative interactions and, ipso facto, arguments involve a variety of goals. Included will always be certain personal (ego or face) goals, as well as goals pertaining to the relationship existing between the arguers. This is completely aside from the task or strategic goal that may (or may not) be the actual impetus for the argument. The relevance of goals analysis can be exemplified, to cite one example, in Bavelas (Blacks, Chorils, & Mullet, 1990) where she concluded that better, more sophisticated communicators *choose to use* equivocation in situations rather than hurt someone's feelings or seem disagreeable. On this model, failure to disagree directly and state one's position outright is not an instance of the "fallacy" of equivocation or even of poor argumentation technique, but the sign of a sophisticated communicator treading lightly in an awkward context.

Feminist Concerns

There is a final tributary to recent developments in Argumentation Theory that requires mention. In 1983, Moulton published an article critical of the "adversary method" she saw as the basic model of philosophical disputation. This view was echoed and amplified by Warren in 1988 when she argued that the core "conceptual framework" on which philosophical (and other high-level) argumentation is based is essentially patriarchal, inimical to women, and designed to aid in the suppression of women. Nye (1990) in her history of logic, *Words of Power*, also concluded that the linear, abstract modes of thought that value the following of rules above all else, exclude women and other groups that are either not privy to the educative process necessary, or whose own makeup, psychology, and sociology do not lend themselves to the dominant white Euro-male reasoning structures. Finally, Tannen (1990), a communication theorist, detailed how different the natural processes women rely on are from those men find congenial. The result is, at the very least, a difficulty in understanding and communicating across gender lines.

Although the claims made are controversial even within the feminist community, the results of the arguments brought by the anti-linearity feminist writers at least means that traditional assumptions must be questioned. If the rules and procedures that have historically been taught by the Informal Logicians are exclusionary and do make argument easier for (many) men than for (most) women, then an injustice exists. Moreover, there is the distinct likelihood that patterns thought to be natural or basic may only be so to one group or another, thus resulting once again in the localization of rules for argument or, at the very least, the expansion of techniques and the alteration of key definitions. Traditional ideology holds, for example, that a good argument is a strong one that effectively eliminates or at least dramatically weakens, an opposer's stand. On several models, though, this approach severely lacks ingredients considered by some to be crucial. An opposer's feelings, ego, the future relationship between proponent and opponent, and the continuation of agreeable discourse are all factors (to name but a few) that might intervene to mediate just what is 'good' and what is not.

The New Outlook

Rightly or wrongly, there has been, since Aristotle, a separation between logic, dialectic, and rhetoric. In various ways, this is mirrored in the separation of mind and body, and the division of arguments into those that persuade and those that convince. Informal Logic, since its inception, has been primarily concerned with the inculcation of values and techniques that are seen to belong to dialectic, to convincing, as opposed to rhetoric which is seen as a dealing with (mere) persuasion. As a result, certain very human factors such as emotion and intuition have been viewed as extraneous to proper argumentation and solely the domain of other disciplines (Psychology and Communication Theory,) or, worse, the concern of sophists and manipulators. In addition, the focus has been on the examination of arguments in isolation from their context and the social, political and cultural situation of the arguers.[8]

The difficulty with such a narrow view was that it created an image of humanity that is overly barren and sterile. Human beings change their beliefs interactively, that is, argue, in a multitude of ways only some of which rely exclusively or primarily upon patterns of reasoning that can be identified and categorized. What has been happening in Argumentation Theory is the realization that this is not wholly bad. Emotion, intuition, and physicality are not plagues that stalk the land of Reason, but perfectly natural and ordinary components of all human endeavor. Today, the classical Informal Logician is having difficulty ignoring the developments in correlative fields that deal with the various modes in which people communicate that do not neatly fall within the category of "rational." The current trends in Argumentation Theory and Communication Theory go a long way toward viewing arguers as persons who are arguing, rather than out-of-context actors performing exercises in appropriately logico-rational behavior. Journals such as *Informal Logic, Argumentation and Advocacy,* and *Argumentation* draw more and more on and attract an interdisciplinary audience. Recent conferences see critical reasoning advocates, who believe arguments need to be stripped of all non-rational "debris," rubbing shoulders with social scientists who believe no argument can be understood in isolation from its social and cultural situation. It is the move toward the integration of these approaches that is having a major impact on the field. The cross-pollination is a result of distinct groups sharing similar concerns: How can we understand and improve the basic human activity of argumentation?

It may well be that the goal of creating an idol of rationality toward which we must all strive is both unrealistic and unnatural. I also believe that it is a mistake to try and deny and/or denigrate those aspects of argumentation that do not meet the standards of Informal Logic as characterized by traditional critical-rationalist proponents. Recent events in Argumentation Theory, it seems to me, are moving the field in a more inclusive direction by bringing the concerns of related disciplines to bear upon the issues Informal Logic has traditionally dealt with. I firmly believe this is all to the good.

Perelman and Toulmin began with a dissatisfaction with formal logic as a model for the practice of argumentation. Following on their heels numerous scholars made contributions toward an understanding of argumentation as a human process. It is not just the social scientists who see argument as taking place in a context, but the Informal Logicians as well. When Kahane (1971) updated the examples of classical

---

[8]I do not count a 20 word background accompanying a newspaper quote as a sufficient explication of context or situation.

fallacies so as to create "relevance" for contemporary students, he was part of an inexorable move from the formal to the natural that can, nonetheless, utilize formalization as representation as opposed to idealization. This continuation will inevitably result in the advancement of our knowledge of argumentation, as well as its hopefully replacing violence as a tool for moving people from one belief to another.

2

The Delimitation of Argument

One of the major issues facing argumentation theorists concerns the range of human communicative interactions that will be covered by the term 'argument.' If the definition agreed upon is too narrow, then we remain mired in technical studies lacking practical utility to acting individuals. If the term is too broad, then, potentially, every human action becomes an argument, and Argumentation Theory disappears, swallowed whole by the social sciences. The fact that the term 'argument' lies at the heart of Argumentation Theory does not mean that there is any consensus as to the correct meaning or use of the term. The sense of the term 'argument' used is a function of the theory adopted by the user. Needs and prejudices from the different perspectives of each contributory discipline, as well as academic disagreements in disciplines, means that each theory relies on a distinct, although related, sense of the term, some of which involve terminological conflict while others do not. In other words, the theory itself and the approach on which it is founded, defines a sense of the term 'argument' appropriate to its needs. Nonetheless, most definitions offered by argumentation theorists, whether Informal Logicians, Communication Theorists, or something between, fall into one of three camps. Five definitions that neatly fall into the first two of these camps will be examined. In addition, a sixth definition will be presented based primarily on ordinary usage, but also incorporating the approach found in the Communication Theory subarea of Discourse Analysis.

The essential issue faced here is the delimitation of the concept 'argument.' The question may be phrased as follows: Which sorts of communicative interactions are to be considered as arguments and which are not? The answer to this question determines what argumentation scholars should study and what they can ignore. This is especially important because many scholars use argument as an honorific that indicates a certain minimal level of intellectual activity beneath which a communicator need not be heeded. As a result, the designation of a particular type of activity as non-argument means that the messages contained therein may be ignored or, at least, dealt with in a way less respectful than "real argumentation." The aim of this chapter is to argue for a broad definition of the term 'argument.'

Defining Argument

There are many terms that can be applied to dialogic communications that subdivide the generic classification 'argument.' Walton (1990) offered a taxonomy that covers a wide range of categories. Unfortunately, only a small subset of these categories are considered by most researchers to be worthy of the attention of critical reasoning researchers. Moreover, the assumption in such a taxonomy is that the categories are separable and that, for example, a "quarrel" can be distinguished from a "critical discussion." This leads to a ranking relying first on explicitness and secondly on logico-critical content. Invariably, the natural argument must be stripped and refined in order that the "underlying argument" be exposed. In other words, for the members of the first view, the "real argument" is something that is ideally presented in a clear and linear fashion, and, at worst, must be extricated from the mare's nest of emotional and psychological debris in which it is found.

The first camp accounts for the first two of the six definitions to be listed in the following sections, and is represented by the Informal Logicians Ralph Johnson, J. Anthony Blair, and Trudy Govier. The definitions offered by these scholars narrow the notion of argumentation to a procedure that is precise and contained. The approach appeals to rules and procedures, relies heavily on the analysis of components, and invariably winnows arguments down from complex, sometimes heated exchanges to sets of premises, conclusions, moves, and counter-moves. Indeed, this refining of arguments from rough and tumble discourse to their distilled logico-rational essence is the *raison d'être* of this approach. I refer to the definitions offered by this group as the *Dialectical view.*

The second perspective, represented here by Charles Willard and myself, sees argument as not necessarily so well-structured. Rather, it is a loose, sometimes "anything goes," communicative dynamic, the main focus of which is the notion of disagreement. Arguments, on this view, are not identified by how one goes about having them, but by what causes or impels them. As a result, there may be a dearth of analytical tools available for argument investigation insofar as arguments, as opposed to one *aspect* of them, cannot really be standardized. This approach is called the *Rhetorical view.*

So far, we have two extremes, especially if we are considering the notion of inclusiveness as central to the definition. That is, the rhetorical view includes many more occasions of dialogic interaction as argument than does the dialectical view. Falling in-between these two, but, perhaps, closer to the dialetical approach is the Amsterdam School of Pragma-Dialectics led by Frans van Eemeren and Rob Grootendorst. Their utilization of actual argumentation and detailed analysis of recorded examples makes their approach broader than a strictly dialetical one, but their commitment to reason and limitation on forms of communication ultimately puts them in that camp, albeit at the left-wing.

A last definition, not yet classified, is due to Scott Jacobs and Sally Jackson, and represents the approach taken in Discourse Analysis, which views argumentation as a disruption to the successful flow of conversation. On the Discourse Analytic view an argument is something to be fixed or corrected in order that the conversation may continue in a mutually agreeable way. The Discourse Analysis approach is conjoined with ordinary usage which, I claim, holds that the term 'argument' has an essentially *negative* element. (This will be amplified in the following section.) These two groups will be labeled the Ordinary View.[9]

To outrageously capsulize, then, the Dialectical view holds that 'argument' refers to a form of communication that involves several precise intellectual steps; the Rhetorical view maintains that 'argument' refers generally to situations in which different opinions are allegedly or actually in contest; and the ordinary view holds that argument is an essentially negative communicative interaction. The six definitions will now be presented, and the ordinary view will then be discussed in more detail.

Six Definitions of Argument

1. Johnson and Blair (1987): Argument is a dialectical process involving the presentation of a position involving the offering and answering of questions relevant to the acceptance of a proposition (pp. 45–46).
2. Govier (1987): "An ... argument is ... a piece of discourse or writing in which someone tries to convince others (or himself) of the truth of a claim by citing reasons on its behalf" (p. 4).
3. van Eemeren, Grootendorst: "Argumentation is a verbal and social activity of reason aimed at increasing (or decreasing) the acceptability of a controversial standpoint for the listener or the reader, by putting forward a constellation of propositions intended to justify (or refute) the standpoint before a rational judge" (van Eemeren, Grootendorst, & Snoeck Henkemans, 1996, p. 7).
4. Willard (1990): "*Argument* is a form of interaction in which two or more people maintain what they construe to be incompatible positions" (p. 1).
5. Gilbert (1996): "An argument is any disagreement—from the most polite discussion to the loudest brawl" (p. 5).
6. Jacobs and Jackson (1980): "arguments are disagreement relevant speech events" based on a disruption in the desired response in a conversation (p. 254).

The Ordinary View

The first three definitions stress the ideas of logico-rational acceptance, the exchange of reasons, and being convinced through the use of language. Definitions 4 and 5 focus on the *fact* of disagreement as opposed to *how* the disagreement

---

[9]The Pragma-Dialectic approach derives from the Communication Theory discipline of Discourse Analysis, and might, therefore, be placed in the same camp. However, the pragma-dialecticians rely on a strong sense of reason that the discourse analysts do not, and, at the same time, the discourse analysts have the element of negativity crucial to the Ordinary view.

proceeds; any action performed in the context of the disagreement is an argument. The sixth definition also has as its essence the notion that since something has happened, namely disagreement, the conversation consequently requires repair. The presence of argument, according to the sixth definition, indicates that the conversation has gone wrong, and needs fixing. Adding this sense of negativity, of wrongness, precludes this definition's simple inclusion into the Rhetorical view, and, instead, places it in the ordinary view which is intended to capture the ordinary language sense of the term. Definitions 1 through 3 use 'argument' as an honorific; the term is applied to a process that is characterized by reason, creative interaction, thoughtfulness, and is explicitly verbal (or at least straightforwardly verbalisable.) Definitions 4 and 5 cover many more situations, but also fail to capture the generally *negative* association most ordinary language users apply to the English term 'argument.' When asking ordinary people what they think about argument, my personal (and unscientific) experience is that about 15% of respondents will state, "I love to argue." Another 15% will say something like, "Oh, I never argue." Members of these two groups are at the extremes. The majority explain that they do not like to argue, but will not go to great lengths to avoid it, and allow that it has useful and important social and relational functions. If pursued, the interlocutor will be told that the individual questioned prefers *discussions*, but not arguments. Indeed, on the ordinary view arguments are not usually the sort of thing one enjoys.[10]

It is certainly the case that the term 'argument' can be used in a multitude of ways, by theorists and ordinary users alike. However, most of the time most language users, i.e., people, associate the term 'argument' with a *negative conflictual experience charged with emotion*. This means that there is 1] disagreement between the communicating parties; 2] the disagreement goes beyond the level of calm and cool discussion; and 3] emotions flare and simmer during the interaction. In this sense of the term, arguments are often considered to be unfortunate, albeit unavoidable, interactions. Even in those situations where argument is to be expected, e.g., sensitive meetings and intimate relationships, it is frequently viewed with trepidation and distaste. 'Argument' as used in the general population, contains within it the notions of anger and heated opposition, emotions most people prefer to avoid. Argument theorists, on the other hand, do not think of argument in this negative way. Since the theorists use the term more narrowly and more technically, they focus on the logical, critical, and rational value of argument. This means that theorists often have to defend argument and explain why it is a benevolent, vital, and sometimes enjoyable component of human interaction and communication. Doing this involves explaining that one does not have to use 'argument' to just mean a fight. Nonetheless, most non-academic respondents do view the term 'argue' negatively, and talking about a "good argument," of the sort so beloved by academics, is considered at worst an oxymoron, and at best an unusual occurrence.

---

[10]While no documentation exists for these figures, they are based on 20 years of asking students and clients for their reactions to various terms such as 'argument,' 'discussion,' 'quarrel,' and so on. The claim is, therefore, experiential and not statistical.

(The general public reserves the term 'discussion' for dissensual interactions it does not find negative.) This negative attitude toward argument can be underscored by presenting several familiar expressions:

> "I don't want to argue about it."
> "If all you want to do is argue, then ... "
> "Why do we always end up arguing?"
> "You always argue with everything I say."
> "Let's not argue."

The familiarity of these turns of phrase shows that many people are *argument* avoiders, though not *discussion* avoiders. For these people, expressions like, "That was a good argument," or, "I'm glad we had that argument," may indicate surprise and relief, as opposed to the feeling of having had a good workout that, say, an academic might intend. And, replacing the term 'argument' in the above with the term 'discussion' does not produce a set of statements that ring as familiar. One might say, "I don't want to discuss it any further;" but that indicates a frustration with the way the discussion went, not with a distaste for discussions *qua* discussions. Another indicator of the pervasiveness of this attitude, as well as the way the terms 'argument' and 'discussion' are differentiated, can be found in an elementary school teacher's lesson book. In this book, which is concerned with providing lessons for teachers instructing in basic social and life skills, an argument is bad while a discussion is good. There are line drawings showing that children "arguing" are cross and angry, while children "discussing" are pleasant and mild-mannered (Mannix, 1991). This attitude is expressed in definition 7, the ordinary view:

> 7. Ordinary Usage: An argument is a conflictual experience charged with emotion where opposing beliefs, desires and/or attitudes are involved.

The core term here is 'conflict,' which denotes negative situations most people would prefer to avoid. The argument need not follow any particular pattern. It can range from a shouting match or lover's quarrel at one extreme, but might also be a relatively calm interaction with strong undercurrents of emotional tension. What is required is that there is dissensus with regard to something one of the partners feels, believes or wants, and that the level of conflict rises above the partners' comfort level.[11] On the other hand, two partners sitting down to calmly work out their differences or make a difficult decision on which they do not see eye to eye would not be described as "arguing" unless the "discussion" got out of hand. In that instance they may have originally been described as "just talking," but the discussion might be said to have *degenerated* into an argument.

---

[11]There may be some cultural differences relevant here. In some cultures what is here described as 'arguing' may not be considered really negative. That may be reserved for *fighting*. The differences follow through *mutatis mutandis*.

The Definitions Compared

The ordinary view, [7], is allied to the Discourse Analysis view, [6], because they both have at their core the idea that argument is a disruption in an otherwise smooth flowing interaction. But the sixth view also connects to the Rhetorical view because it views argument as essentially motivated by disagreement rather than identifying it by its processes. Consequently, this view has connections to both the Ordinary and Rhetorical stands.

The relation between definitions 1 to 3, namely, the Dialectical view, and definition [7] is instructive because there is a definite intersection between them. There are arguments that fall under the umbrella of the Ordinary usage that are Dialectical arguments and those that are not. That is, to the Dialecticians, the interaction in question qualifies as an argument if, *regardless of the level of emotion*, physicality and empathy, it meets the minimal requirements of being reasoned, dialectic and focused.[12] It should thus be clear that I am in no way suggesting that the Dialecticians outlaw the less cerebral aspects of communication, but rather that they do not see any of them as necessary or even vital concomitants of argumentation. To the contrary, the role such aspects of communication play is potentially harmful to good argumentation. Some Dialecticians would put a limit on the amount or degree of emotion, etc. present in the interchange such that exceeding that limit means the interchange is not an argument, but something else such as a squabble or quarrel. Still, many instances of argumentation that are Ordinary-acceptable would also be Dialectical-acceptable. For the Dialecticians, it is not necessary to be arguing without any emotion or excitement, just that those aspects must be under control and not the overriding force of the encounter.

The Rhetorician's definition, on the other hand, does cover all instances of ordinary argument, but then also goes on to include many more types of interaction that would not be called arguments on the Ordinary view. In particular, the Rhetorical view includes all the Dialectical instances rejected by the Ordinary view on the grounds that they are not at all emotionally charged. The Rhetoricians, like the Dialecticians, do not *require* emotion, but unlike the Dialecticians, also do not deem as necessary any form of logico-rational processes. According to both the Dialectical and Rhetorical views, arguments can have a nondispassionate nature where the purpose is inquiry and the persons involved remain calm, emotionally disinterested, and use (by and large) careful, linear, logical, step-by-step reasoning. We will refer to non-emotional argumentative exchanges of this nature as *clinical* arguments. This is preferable to, say, 'rational,' as it avoids the suggestion that emotional exchanges are, *ipso facto*, non-rational. Using this terminology we can now state that, on the Ordinary view, clinical dialogic arguments are often called 'discussions.' They are viewed as interesting, perhaps challenging, even worth-while and intellectually stimulating, but are not considered 'arguments.' It is, of

---

[12]I do not, of course, mean physicality in the sense of violence, but in the sense of using one's body and surroundings.

course, fascinating that a term considered by the Dialecticians to be an honorific is considered by the Ordinary view to be a derogative.

For the Dialecticians, the Holy Grail is *dialectic*, (or, for the Pragma-Dialecticians, *critical discussion*) that interactive endeavor pursued by Socrates and exemplified in the Platonic dialogues. As an ideal, it is careful, disinterested, dedicated to the search for truth, and devoid of ego involvement and intentional misdirection. Dialectic is the paragon of argumentation, the way it should be conducted if we are to truly better ourselves and remain above the quagmire from which we evolved. Dialectic, and its monological correlate, are what should be included under the rubric 'argument.' Unstructured exchanges not proceeding in an orderly manner that involves the presentation and questioning of a position and its objections are eschewed by the Dialecticians because the position on which the exchange is focused may not be articulated or even articulatable. That is, the premises and conclusion may not be easily or practically identifiable. For the Rhetorical and the Ordinary user the plaint, "We argue all the time, but I never know what we're arguing about," requires no correction. The Dialectician, on the other hand, would require a change to some such term as 'fight,' 'row' or 'quarrel.' If you do not know what you are arguing about then you are not arguing, you are doing something else. To argue just means to have a conclusion and premises that form a position that can be identified, questioned, attacked and defended.

The arguments eschewed by the Dialecticians do not have the requisite parts, or, at least, not all of them. Worse yet, all the parts might be there, *but no one is paying any attention to them*. The partners to the dispute are too caught up in their emotions, egos, feelings, or what have you, to listen to the statements being put forward and notice how they impact on their own position. Such arguments will hereafter be called *chaotic*, and they are to be thought of as opposed to dialectical arguments. Note that a "chaotic argument" is not one that has no structure, but rather one where the statements and responses made by the disputants do not necessarily relate to each other, and where there is not usually reasonably careful attention to question and answer. In a chaotic argument it can be very difficult to determine just who is defending what, and the participants themselves may be (a) unclear about what the issue is, and (b) wrong as to their dispute partner's position on the issue. Both parties will agree that there is some disagreement, but it might as easily be of attitude or feeling as of belief.

Types of Arguments

There are now two measures that can be applied to various interactions that enable us to see how the three uses of the term 'argument' are applied. The first measure is the emotional–clinical continuum, and the second is the dialectical–chaotic continuum. In the following, in order to avoid pre-judgment, the generic term 'dispute' will be used to cover the broadest possible sense of the term 'argument.' Which disputes are arguments depends on which view/usage one holds, and may be represented by Table 2.1.

TABLE 2.1
Types of Arguments

	Emotional	Clinical
	Rhetorical	Rhetorical
Dialectical	Dialectical	Dialectical
	Ordinary	
	Rhetorical	
Chaotic	Ordinary	Rhetorical

Several points arising from this chart are worth noting. The first is that no group believes that emotion precludes argument. While only Ordinary users make emotion a necessary condition of argument, both Rhetoricians and Dialecticians still expect it to commonly be present. Johnson and Blair (1983) specifically set aside the emotion versus reason dichotomy (p. 171), and Govier (1987) seems concerned with the quantity of emotive language rather than its simple presence (p.121–122). This is not to say that there is no connection between emotionality and chaos. I believe most of us would agree that as emotional pitch tends to rise so does the likelihood of chaos, although not in any necessary correlation.

Of course, none of this need be a problem for Argumentation Theory. It would be the simplest thing to create a nomenclature that would respect all three terminologies. Wenzel (1980) suggested that argumentation should be divided into three perspectives: process, product, and procedure. Process covers the rhetorical aspect, product the logical, and procedure the dialectical. By paying attention to which perspective is under consideration, researchers will avoid thinking they are talking about argumentation in general, and not step on each other's toes or engage in jurisdictional disputes.

Wenzel is correct in suggesting that some differences can be resolved this way. What a dialectician means by 'argument' is just not what a rhetorician means by the term. There is, therefore, a temptation to define away the problem by designating different terms for different activities. 'Dispute,' for example, might be used to cover the Rhetoricians' interpretation, and include anything anyone might loosely consider to be an argument. 'Formal dialectic' could be assigned to the Dialecticians to designate arguments that are sufficiently dialectical, and 'quarrel' could be assigned to those arguments normally identified by the term 'argument' in Ordinary usage. Notwithstanding that the terms suggested overlap in various ways, this Solomonaic path of no resistance still leaves one major question unanswered. What is it that Argumentation Theory should study? And, for that matter, what sorts of arguments should philosophers, argumentation theorists or not, consider, respect, study and teach? The Ordinary usage will not do; it utilizes emotional conflict in an inappropriate way insofar as it *requires* that disputes be emotional before they qualify as arguments. Certainly, Argumentation Theory will not exclude clinical and dialectical arguments. Whether they are put forward as paradigms or not, they are, at the very least, important sorts of arguments for those who appreciate their beauty and nuance. Argumentation theory cannot want to separate emotional from clinical arguments *for the purpose of determining the field's domain of study.* No philosopher believes that all arguments are, can be, or should be, devoid of emotion, but Ordinary usage insofar as it *requires* a minimal emotional and conflictual component in disputes is unsuitable as a definition.

The Dialectical approach, however, suffers from exactly the opposite extreme. There seems to be just too many dialogic interchanges that most people label as argumentative to ignore the discrepancy. The difficulty stems from the Dialecticians' admiration of logico-rationality, usually just called 'reason' and invariably put forward as the mode of communication most appropriate for settling differences of opinion. Unfortunately, this neglects the fact that human beings communicate on many different levels, not just the verbal and intellectual. Other modes of reasoning are available and utilized regularly in practically every conceivable circumstance and most certainly in argumentation (see chapter 6).

It is no accident that the Dialectical and Ordinary senses of 'argument' have one crucial aspect in common. They both use 'argument' normatively. The Ordinary view's connotation of the term is negative, and indicates an unpleasant situation that, at the least, could be handled better. For the Dialecticians, however, the connotation is positive and allows that the situation might have been handled in the best possible way. At the very least, the parties put forward claims and reasons in their support and examined each others' sub-arguments with a logico-rational critical eye. On this account, according to the Dialecticians, the interaction that begins with, "You left the car out of gas again this morning," and ends with mutual recriminations is just not an argument. It is simply not about the subject that the words in the argument make it sound like it is about. There may even be agreement that the implicit position in the above may be construed as, "You ought not leave the car without gas." But for the Dialectician, what is important about the counter, "Big deal, you forgot to put the garbage out," is that it can be interpreted as an instance of the *tu quoque* fallacy.[13] The rejoinder, in other words, is strictly viewed as responding to claim, warrant, or backing rather than as one person responding to another in a particular situation. If the next round is even "worse," e.g., "Oh, yeah, well then the heck with you," then the partners to the dispute most definitely cannot be said to be having an argument.

The Rule of the Linguistic

Most observers, certainly Ordinary and Rhetorical, would agree that there clearly is the beginning of an argument, *dialectical or otherwise*, commencing in the example just given. But the Dialectician cannot allow this. Allowing it means the denial of the supremacy of language in the pantheon of communication. It means

---

[13]The Pragma-Dialectic program is moving in a direction that allows for more latitude in analyzing statements for the role they play as well as the words they contain. See, for example, pp. 96–100 of van Eemeren, Grootendorst, Jacobs, and Jackson (1993).

that the linguistically explicit is not always the first and last appeal, that is, arguments cannot be won only because of what someone said. And this is the very heart of the dialectical position: what makes it conservative is that it only permits as argumentatively significant those processes that are observable, identifiable, and that follow certain rules and procedures. To do otherwise is just to do something other than argue.

No Dialectician actually maintains that every part of an argument must be linguistically explicit. Enthymemes are taken for granted as the normal way to communicate, but note that almost all the techniques for determining the enthymematic elements rest on the assumption that there is a quasi-linguistic element that can somehow be uncovered. It is as if the very proposition is hiding in some Gricean mind and can be levered out with a modus ponens. The Dialectician does not require the linguistically explicit, but the linguistically *explicable* to use D. J. O'Keefe's 1982 terminology. The dispute must be capable of being put into language. Why? Because if there is no requirement for linguistic explicability, then we do not know what we are talking about when we dispute, and *ipso facto* it is not argument. There is no way out of this for the Dialectical view.

There are two difficulties with this position. The first difficulty is that the problems of identifying enthymematic premises in a noncontroversial and generally agreed on way is notoriously difficult (see, Gilbert, 1991). Arguments, moreover, do not even have to be enthymematic to create problems with interpretation or comprehension. Just consider the controversies that have arisen about the way in which one scholar portrays the work of another. Professor Smith writes a 500 page book, and Professor Jones first summarizes it in several paragraphs and then proceeds to attack it. Professor Smith, as everyone expects, explains that Professor Jones completely misunderstood her. The simple fact is that, regardless of the level of explicitness and certainly allowing for questions of degree, written and verbal arguments are *always* open to various interpretations. When the situation is, as it normally is, not linguistically explicit, then we must interpret and draw on nonverbal aspects of a message in order to understand it. The point is not that we cannot understand each other, but that, amazingly enough, we do. We do communicate with a remarkable degree of comprehension; but comprehension must not be confused with precision. Precision comes from the interaction of communicators working together to understand, not from the simple presence of linguistic elements or the sole reliance on logico-rational techniques. While this is recognized in the Pragma-Dialectic approach, even there the goal is to *bring precision* to the encounter by utilizing the transformation rules to create a reconstruction. But normal methods of becoming clear do not rely so much on logical analysis as on other, more inclusive methods.

The second difficulty is this. Understanding another person's point of view requires more than getting right the meanings of the words being used. Communication does not even occur with words, but with messages that use words as one aspect of their communicative shell. Words, most especially when used in dialogic situations, do not give the entire message, but only part of it. The remainder, which may vary from a small percentage to practically the entire communication, is embedded in the context, tonality, history, and personalities of the arguers. Without all this, with words alone, we do not have sufficient information to disambiguate the simplest message, let alone a complex argument. To cite a simple example, consider the following.

Snowstorm   (2.1)

> Jill stands next to her husband, Jack, and looks out the window at the huge piles of snow completely blocking the street. "Great," she says, "I can't get to work today."

This statement can mean either that she is happy she has a day off, or that she is upset that she cannot get into the office. Her husband, Jack, standing beside her, will, in all likelihood, know which she means—even if her voice was flat. According to Grice (1989), we make conversational sense of those things that do not jibe with our normal understanding. We bring more to language than our comprehension of specific words. Language only carries part of meaning. But note that only someone like Jack, who knows how Jill feels about her job, will have sufficient information to properly unpack the conversational implicature.

In Praise of the Rhetorical

The aforementioned considerations are certainly not revolutionary, but they seem not to have permeated the Dialectical approach to argumentation as held by the Informal Logicians. For them, the words are everything and the rest is winnowed, eliminated and discarded. But this simply will not work. In order to understand a particular argumentation, we must bring to it considerable information not presented in the actual words. Simply put, the choices are to give up the assumption that we know things at all, or allow that we know things without the exclusive use of language. This is because we *do* know what people mean when they say things, and we must admit that the knowledge of that meaning does not come exclusively from understanding the language of the message. Ergo, it comes from other modes of communication.

The Ordinary view is also incapable of performing as a standard definition insofar as it excludes too many arguments both the Dialecticians and Rhetoricians want included and that have been included for millennia. Simply put, the Ordinary view cannot exclude arguments that do not involve conflict or negative experience, since ordinary language allows that there are such things as "good arguments," "interesting arguments," and so on. But this means that all those communicative events are, *ipso facto*, arguments, just as spicy food is, *ipso facto*, food. In other words, there are interactions that are both non-conflictual and positive. Consequently, the Ordinary view will be taken into consideration, but will not be adopted as nomenclature appropriate for delimiting Argumentation Theory.

The most basic difference between the Dialectical and Ordinary views as compared to the Rhetorical view, is the latter's lack of normativity.[14] For the first two views, the most important consideration is that argument is considered in a certain light, positive for the former and negative for the latter. The Rhetorical approach is not to judge the argument, but to understand the position it represents, not to set out rules and procedures, but to discover rules and procedures. In order to do this, argumentation must first be observed as a process, and the emphasis must be shifted from the argu*ment* to the argu*er*. When this is finished, we can examine the process as an attempt to attain certain goals or accomplish certain ends, and then we can inspect this process from various perspectives including the logical, critical, psychological, sociological, and moral. One important difference is that we are then in a position to isolate the perspective most germane to the particular proceedings, rather than apply one set of criteria across the board. Moreover, we resist the attempt to co-opt 'argument' for one of the several perspectives, or even, as the more liberal Pragma-Dialectic School does, identify 'good argument' with one form of argumentation, namely, critical inquiry.

The other advantage to the Rhetorical view is that it does not limit argumentative moves. Anything can happen in an argument and still be considered part of it. Views such as this have been propounded by Brockriede and Willard (1989). Brockriede (1975) says, "people will find arguments in the vicinity of people." Willard goes further:

> I prefer to avoid a priori requirements for the utterance to be found in arguments except that arguers, like all communicators, employ the full range of available communication modalities, verbal and nonverbal, explicit and implicit. The theory defended here thus defines argument in terms of encounters based on dissensus and regards any communications occurring therein as objects of epistemic and critical interest. (p. 8)

When there is disagreement, people will engage in many diverse activities designed variously to persuade, win, investigate, placate, convince, intimidate, or whatever is called for by the particular dissensual context. The mistake is not in investigating one of these techniques. The mistake lies in attempting to limit the notion of argument to only one of these several possible avenues. It is not that the logico-rational approach to Argumentation Theory is wrong as much as that it is not the only approach.

The Rhetorical view is inclusive; it does not preclude any particular approach or discipline from having important input into Argumentation Theory. Since it begins with observation rather than instruction, it must be open to any sort of analysis that might shed light on the process. The subject of investigation is the determination of exactly what goes on in an argument, not what *should* go on in an argument. As a result, and as most participants in arguments know, a wide range of human activity is covered. And, the use of the term 'human' here is not accidental.

---

[14]This is not to say that there are theories without normative aspects, but rather that the Dialectical and Ordinary views have a much higher normative component that the Rhetorical.

The Dialectical view, with its emphasis on a logico-rational model, works by eliminating what the model cannot handle. If the input is not intelligible to the processor, then it is eschewed. But forsaking one model in favor of a multiplicity means that anything that actually occurs in an argument (broadly considered) can be analyzed, itemized, dissected, and judged. It is the embrasure of the human-ness of argumentation that makes the Rhetorical view so attractive. At one and the same time it is accepting and analytical. It accepts whatever occurs as just that—an argumentative occurrence, while in no way precluding analysis and judgment, provided only that said normative elements are clearly and openly demarcated and (ideally) defended.

There is a further advantage to the Rhetorical position, namely, it is much more amenable to alternative modes of reasoning. There are those who claim that the traditional logico-rational approach is culture and or gender specific. Grice (1989), for example, identified a set of rules that are clearly derived from a relatively narrow cultural tradition.[15] While Grice's rules might be applicable in differing cultural situations, *mutatis mutandis*, it might be the case that a good deal of stretching might be required to save anything but his broadest notions. Anyone who has had contact with a variety of cultures knows that, in some, arguing calmly and politely may be taken as a sign of disinterest. In some cultures, arguing at all is a gross violation of etiquette, whereas in others, saying only that which needs be said can be a sign of rude taciturnity. Moreover, there are numerous situations in which speaking directly to the point can be damaging to the communication at hand as well as socially unacceptable. In a similar vein, we can consider arguments brought by some feminist scholars. (See chapter 4 for an extensive discussion of this issue.)

The Rhetorical view, unlike the Dialectical does not eschew the category of chaotic–emotional arguments. This is taken to be a benefit, as relatively few arguments seem to lack one or both of these characteristics. On the contrary, if one is to seriously consider the level of chaos and emotion in most of the arguments one comes across on a routine basis, far more would fall into this category than any other. What advantage is there to philosophy to exclude the chaotic and/or the emotional from the court of argumentation? Emotion is as important as logic or rationality to argument, and it is also inextricable from the logic of the argument. There is not some visible delineation between logic and emotion (or intuition or anything else) that allows the scholar to examine one to the exclusion of the other.

Consider what it means to persuade someone of a proposition *P*. First, it must be embraced by them as part of their belief set—and not merely intellectually. Believing on the rational level alone is not sufficient for persuasion. In order for someone to be persuaded of a proposition *P*, that person must change not only his/her belief states but the corresponding attitudes as well. Someone whose mind has been convinced, but does not fully believe, is liable to say something like, "I guess you're right, but I'm still having trouble with it." One can begin with either the mind or the body, but persuasion does not occur until both are synchronized.

---

[15]These considerations have been brought to my attention by several different classes of my third-year argumentation theory at York University.

It is simply wrong for philosophers to ignore the emotional, physical, and intuitional aspects of belief, persuasion, and argumentation. The myth of the rational is not just its elevation to the pinnacle of philosophical importance, but the very idea that it is at all separable from the non-rational in the first place. In studiously avoiding the chaotic-emotive category of argument, Informal Logic isolates itself from its constituency. The very premiss of contemporary critical reasoning is that everything must be defended, justified, and explicated without recourse to situational or contextual or personal information, and while there has recently been a softening of this stand, the core view that argument must be pursued in an orderly and reasonable manner is still strongly entrenched. True, in the heavily discourse analysis influenced Pragma-Dialectic approach, one can work with a relatively chaotic argument, but the task of that working is to form it into a structure identifiable as a critical inquiry. It may be found in a natural state, but is then molded into an object meeting the purposes of the investigator. The ideology is that an argument is an artifact, a thing that can be examined, categorized and judged in isolation from its surroundings like a shell found on the beach. But even then, to understand the nature of the shell its point of discovery must be known. Is it saltwater or fresh? Sandy beach or rocky? The point for Informal Logic should *not* be to improve the reasoning of those who will follow the rules, but rather to find the rules of those whose reasoning needs improving.

Studying an argument is like studying anything else. It is attached and connected to its surroundings in an irrevocable way. There are significant aspects of language, usage, and style that are beyond the comprehension of anyone not familiar with the particular history of those involved. But this does not mean that the analysis of arguments from a multitude of perspectives is a worthless endeavor. Not at all. It is rather that the categories must be extended to include errors, forms, and categories that go beyond the logico-rational and include, systematically, all the modalities of human communication.

Philosophers should not label emotive reasoning, physical actions, and even intuitional communication as not 'argument.' To do so is to write it off as something less than worthy of attention, or, at the least, less ennobling and less important. Certainly this should not be done without, by the Dialectical View's own lights, a very serious argument.

3

Argument and Arguers

An intimate connection exists between Informal Logic and its pedagogical responsibility, Critical Reasoning. These courses, "Critical Reasoning," "Informal Logic," "Modes of Reasoning," and so on, frequently are the mainstay of a philosophy department and are generally well attended and well regarded. Perhaps it is a mistake to complain and want to alter something that seems to be working so well, but that is nonetheless the task of this chapter. I argue that the usual approach taken to critical reasoning is flawed and indicate ways in which the traditional methods can be replaced by a richer, more cooperative approach. The changes needed flow from the Dialectical understanding of argument, as discussed in the previous chapter, and the pedagogical difficulties go hand-in-hand with the aforementioned philosophical difficulties. Simply put, if there is any desire to expand the range of Argumentation Theory to include the sorts of arguments that people actually enter into, then the techniques for analyzing them must be re-examined. This chapter details the ways in which the traditional techniques of Informal Logic fall short of serving real arguers in real situations.

There are two basic problems that will be dealt with in turn. The first is the essentially negative outlook as expressed in the very rubric 'Critical Reasoning;' and the second is the lack of focus on the people who are arguing or who have made the argument under examination. I see both of these problems as instances of the larger issue just raised, namely, the almost total emphasis critical reasoning puts on the argument as an artifact, as opposed to the process of arguing as it occurs between two or more people who are in disagreement. Critical reasoning, it will be argued, does not need to be replaced, but expanded and modified to embrace argu*ers*, and not just argu*ments*.[16]

---

[16]It is very easy to overlook the fact that I am talking about an expansion of critical reasoning and not an elimination of the techniques it already relies on. Nonetheless, I want to emphasize that there is no call here for the abandonment of critical reasoning as it is generally known.

Negativity

One major difficulty with critical reasoning lies in its essential negativity. The way it stands now, the student entering introductory courses in argument analysis is informed, in no uncertain terms, that he is a critic; his job is to look at the argument and criticize it. His purpose is to identify weakness, spot errors, and, generally, to find fault with what has been put before him. We emphasize that criticism is more important than agreement or disagreement. The argument must be taken apart and examined, its nuts and bolts inspected for rust, its belts and cogs tested for worn spots and weak teeth. There *will be* things wrong with the argument and they must be found.[17]

We do, one might respond, have the Principle of Charity, itself in no small part promoted by the strategic importance of meeting your opposer on her best, not weakest, footing. But the strategic aspect aside, the very title of the principle shows its real nature. What it instructs one to give is not support or clarification or defense or insight, but charity. Charity is given to those who are needy, who cannot compose a defensible argument on their own behalf, and who, save for our generous largesse, would appear stupid, shallow, or inept and most certainly be defeated and humiliated. All the Principle of Charity is really intended to do is keep us honest, which means we are actually talking about the *Principle of Honesty*, and that rule one should follow (and teach) as a matter of course.

A given dialectic interchange can have, adapting Perelman's terms, varying degrees of *heuristic* and *eristic* intention. Heuristic intention involves the commitment and effort to look for commonality, agreement, and the truth (even if only the situational truth). *Eristic* intention is the desire to achieve one's strategic ends at all, or at least some, moral costs if necessary. That is, the strategic objective is more important than the methods used to obtain it. Both extremes are constructs, and will actually be found in varying degrees in different dialogues (Perelman & Olbrechts-Tyteca, 1958/1969, p. 37). Expanding on this distinction, the eristic component might be exemplified by insistent urgings or carefully crafted but specious arguments, e.g., arguments which appeal to non-existent statistical data. The heuristic attitude attempts to *understand* an opposer's position before criticizing it. The heuristic attitude is not critical, it is comprehensive. At worst, it deals with agreement and disagreement, not right and wrong. To do critical reasoning properly one must find fault, find not what is right, but what is wrong. The aim is to eliminate the presented argument so that one's own argument can take its place along with the accompanying view. This approach is not heuristic because it is primarily focused on the negative, on the goal of showing an opposer that he or she is wrong.

---

[17]One might argue that the critical aspect is most essential when dealing with one's own arguments, i.e., self-criticism. Indeed, when analyzing one's own arguments one ought be extremely critical. But even here, one ought to make the effort to understand the position's motivation, consequences, goals, and roots as opposed to merely criticizing the structure of the relationship between premises and conclusions. In other words, one certainly can be as critical as one wants with oneself, but still ought to provide oneself with the civil, concerned, and caring attitudes one brings to interactions with others.

It does not put understanding, let alone inclusiveness, at the forefront, but eliminates it in favor of a critical, eristically oriented approach.

Why does critical reasoning have such a negative attitude? Why is the emphasis so heavily slanted toward finding fault with the presented argument? Think of the possibilities if the terminology was changed to, say, "constructive reasoning," or, of course, "coalescent argumentation." We then might be able to tell students that we want to make sense of our opposers' arguments in order to be better equipped to discuss the issues with them. The student could be told to *understand* the argument, to try and determine what her dispute partner means, to find what aspects of the argument she agrees with, what aspects she disagrees with, and how, if at all, the opposing views may be reconciled. To do this, we do not have to throw the baby out with the bath water: there is every reason for a careful arguer to be aware of premises and conclusions, grounds for accepting and rejecting propositions, and, I firmly believe, elementary formal logic in its Natural Deduction guise. It is just that there is more in argumentation than logic, formal or informal, and much of it is systematically discarded, which results in a lack of both comprehension and compassion.

Understanding Arguments

Inculcating a skill means importing techniques, attitudes, and perspectives. It is always difficult, and doing so in a classroom or lecture hall in only two or three hours a week is next to impossible. C. I. Lewis wrote, "Logic is a skill, but reasoning is an art, and as such it cannot be taught." It is, therefore, not surprising that the main approach to critical reasoning has been to formulate rules and procedures that standardize what to look for and how to look for it, i.e., to turn it into a skill. We create categories of mistakes called fallacies and instruct our students to hunt for them. We present rules for connecting statements and teach them to create diagrams that are at best artificial and at worst incomprehensible. The problem is that there seems to be little choice. If there is no focus on the quantifiable, the diagrammable, the structured and regular, then it becomes difficult to know what students will be instructed about. Without being able to appeal to rules and procedures, critical reasoning becomes too particularized; practices and techniques used in one situation may not be applicable to another. As it is impossible to instruct about what to do in *each* given situation, one must generalize away the details until one is left with a structure that is sufficiently identifiable across the board, thus allowing common procedures for *any of this category* of situation.

In symbolic logic, this is exactly what is done. The details of context, language, nuance, purpose, intention, ideology, person, emotion, location, intuition, and truth are stripped away so that a universal structure can be exposed, examined, and placed into a uniform system. When we do this, we explain to our students that this is but one aspect of argument (or language or thought) and that in order to examine it we must, perforce, lose many of the subtleties and nuances that make arguments interesting and worthwhile. In fact, we lose absolutely everything save for the formal logical structure. But that loss is reasonable because there is generally no pretense made about confusing it with reality, and the aridity is necessary to create the model we seek. Even here, when all that is left is a purely abstract structure, there is a great deal of controversy over how a particular argument ought be formalized. It is non-controversial to allow that translation from natural to formal language is not an exact science but, often, a question of interpretation and emphasis. Exactitude escapes us even when we are perfectly willing to pay almost any price.

When it comes to informal logic, the task of identifying the arguments, sub-arguments, premises and conclusions is even more daunting. Now we do not want to lose many of those aspects of communication we were previously willing to sacrifice on the alter of rigor, but, at the same time, we must come up with a formulation of the particular argument that allows us to inspect it with some degree of uniformity and generality. That is, given an argument set on a quiz a class of students should produce an analysis that has recognizably common elements. Once again, this entails ignoring a mass of information that may be highly pertinent to truly understanding the argument. And this leads directly to a crucial question: what does it mean to "understand" an argument?

According to the critical reasoning approach, understanding an argument means that one needs to pare it down to the argumentative essentials. To "sift through the rhetoric," as Johnson and Blair said in the first (1977), second (1983), but not third edition of *Logical Self-Defense*, (1987, p. 80), or according to Govier (1987), to determine which sentences are premises and which sentences conclusions, presumably in both instances discarding the rest (p. 141). But to do this sort of shaving away of "irrelevant" bits and pieces is to fail to look at the argument as a communication, and, therefore, to potentially ignore important if not crucial aspects of the message. The term 'message' is used advisedly: an argument can serve many purposes, only one of which may be to persuade the opposer by purely logico-rational means to the designated conclusion. It may instead (*or as well*) be intended to alert one's partner to certain difficulties, concerns, wonderments, anxieties, and so on. Certainly an argument may be intended to persuade, but it also may be intended to irritate, provoke, test, explore, undermine, upstage, hurt, and so on. The point first mentioned in chapter 2 wants reiteration: Understanding the argument means understanding it *qua* message, as a communication transmitted from one human being to another. To suggest that there is something in there that is "the argument" is as misleading as supposing that there is always one clear way to perform a formal translation. And, the more interesting the argument, the more complex, subtle, and germane it is, the clearer is this simple truth.

Arguments and Arguers

In Informal Logic an argument has one goal: to convince the listener of the truth of the conclusion. That this is the sole or primary goal of argumentation is not, however, a universally acknowledged truth. In contemporary Discourse Analysis, for example, it is axiomatic that every argumentation has several goals. While this will be explored at length in chapter 5, it will suffice here to point out a basic distinction. Some goals can be identified as personal or relationship goals called *face goals* (as per Goffman, 1959, and Brown & Levinson, 1987) and others are identified as *task, target,* or *strategic* goals. In the standard, critical reasoning approach an argument can be "understood" or, if we prefer, "analyzed" independently of the investigation of the goals of the arguers. The very existence of goals is considered completely beside the point. Indeed, if caught looking into the goals of the arguers, one can be charged with some version or other of the genetic fallacy. But how can an action, linguistic or otherwise, really be understood without investigating its intent, its function, and its effects?

The notion of goals and both personal and interpersonal considerations is not idle in understanding arguments. One common observation made of intimate relationships, for example, is that the argument is not really about what it seems to be about. In Informal Logic this makes no sense. Arguments are always about whatever proposition is identified as the conclusion; if it veers from that, then correction and/or critique is required. But this is just wrong. Why should argumentation, unlike any other area of human endeavor, be devoid of subtext, motivation and intent? The answer is that it cannot. To understand an argument is to comprehend its function in a given situation every bit as much as it is to identify its premises and conclusions, indeed, in some contexts even more so. We are right when we acknowledge that the patently silly argument the Smiths had last night about when the salad should be served was not really about proper dinner service.

If we are going to deal with arguments in a more than critical way we need to shift the focus from the argument to the arguer, from the *artifacts* that happen to be chosen for communicative purposes to the *situation* in which those artifacts function as a component. The emphasis, as argued in the previous chapter, is too strongly in favor of language, and language is not nearly as precise as we would like to think it is. We focus on it because it is the only part of the entire argumentative process that is physically identifiable, and even then, many juicy bits are left to our enthymeme-decoding imaginations.[18]

The analysis of each argument must begin by grounding it in its context, in appreciating its source, the goals of its producer, and the aims of the interaction taken as a whole. Even an editorial, let alone discursive dialectic, requires its context and situation. An editorial about the North American Free Trade Agreement (NAFTA) in a pro-union labor oriented newspaper should be read differently from one in a pro-business financially oriented one. Each newspaper has, as it were, a different personality or profile and therefore the background assumptions, implicit claims, ideology, and goals will be different in each case. This is also true of people. What is the relationship between the disputers? The very same words spoken between an employee and employer might have totally different meanings and import than those same words spoken by a wife to her husband. Informal Logicians

---

[18]Any scholar who has ever had his or her position portrayed by a critic knows very well that distortion and emphasis can occur even (giving the benefit of the doubt) with the most honorable intentions.

need to talk about the very same *argument* spoken between different sets of people, but that is a mistake. Just because the same utterances are sounded, the same noises made, does not mean they have the same meaning. Someone leaving a movie theater and responding to the question, "What'd you think of the movie?" may say, "Great," and mean either that it was very good or very lousy.

The point made in the previous chapter was that argument should be defined in such a way as to permit a broad enough definition that the actual argumentative methods used by actual arguers can be included and studied. In this chapter, I have tried to show that the essential negativity and focus on artifacts inherent in the Informal Logic approach leads it away from cooperation and comprehension and toward criticism and arid analysis. If a wider range of arguments are to be included in Argumentation Theory, then Informal Logic must change its focus. Argumentation Theory has an ancient and time-honored connection to the teaching of critical and rhetorical skills. While it is important that the skills traditionally taught continue to be imparted, it is also important that more emphasis be put on the variability of arguments that may even sound and look alike. In addition, as will be argued in the next chapter, there are very strong reasons to consider alternative forms of argumentation as legitimate.

4

Feminism and Argumentation

The criticisms brought against critical reasoning in the previous chapter stem from a view of argumentation that focuses on the situated nature of argument. The position is that the essentially negative and rule-oriented approach is unnecessarily harsh. The values promoted accentuate fault-finding and criticism as the main purpose of argument analysis. But, in addition to these norms, there are other more philosophically potent values as well. These values include a conception of reality that accepts a fairly rigorous sense of the true/false, wrong/right dichotomies, the holding dear of the convince/persuade distinction, and at least some version of the Natural Light Theory. As explained in chapter 1, the convince/persuade distinction holds that the proper way to argue appeals exclusively to reason, logic, and the mind. When an individual changes her mind as a result of the application of these methods she will be said to have been "convinced." Persuasion, on the other hand, appeals to emotion, self-interest, and the body. Being persuaded, as opposed to convinced, is to have changed one's mind by dint of lesser, fallacious, or rationally inappropriate means.

The *Natural Light Theory* is the view that the "true" or "best" position will be the one to survive a properly conducted rational competitive inquiry. This requires that there is a grounded distinction between what is true and what is false, and that, somehow, theories or statements that are true have a greater ability to stand up to critical scrutiny. In addition, this ability to resist criticism is, in some way, noticeable or identifiable. Therefore, true statements/theories/beliefs have a natural light that permits us to identify them.

I call the nexus of values, techniques and attitudes as described in the previous chapter with the additions just mentioned, the *Critical-Logical Model* [hereafter, C-L]. According to the C-L, the best examples of reasoning are linear and careful. Extraneous material such as emotional content, power relationships, and the social consequences of the argument are separated from its text or transcript in order that the *argument* itself can be examined. Discovery and justification are two very separate processes on the C-L view, facts are things we can get our hands on, and the politics, social outlook, or personal history, i.e., the *situation*, of the arguers is almost always irrelevant to the evaluation of the argument. Information is carefully separated into that which is relevant and may be adduced as evidence or reasons, and that which is not and must be ignored or put aside while the argument is being examined.

In what follows, I examine the assumptions and values inherent in the C-L model in light of objections brought by several feminist commentators. In this chapter, I review those objections and examine how they impact on Argumentation Theory. I will argue that the objections are reasonable, that they have a moral basis, and that the conception of coalescent argumentation that forms the core focus of this book works well as a response to these concerns. Very briefly, then, coalescent argumentation posits agreement as the goal of successful argumentation wherein the object is to identify not what is wrong with an argument, but what are the points of agreement and disagreement. The emphasis is on minimizing disagreement by carefully examining what crucially requires disagreement as opposed to what is merely an inessential accompaniment of the opposed position. Furthermore, coalescent argumentation views an argument not as an isolated and autonomous artifact, but as a linguistic representative for a *position-cluster* of attitudes, beliefs, feelings and intuitions. In this regard, coalescent argumentation is an *attitude* correlated to a *practice*. The concept is discussed at great length in succeeding chapters.

Some Preliminary Issues

Several words of caution. The choices laid out here can be viewed as involving a total choice of paradigms, or, at the least, to use Warren's (1988) terminology, conceptual frameworks. As a result, the adjudication process is complex: which mode or tradition shall be used as the criteria for acceptance? Which form(s) of arguing are to be permitted? I have been led in this by two factors. First, my own work (Gilbert, 1994) is strongly based on the importance of eclecticism in reasoning. Secondly, the C-L Principle of Charity instructs us to give as much as we can to an opponent in the interest of logical fairness, but also to prevent an easy getaway. Consequently, where I have had to choose I have chosen to take as wide a latitude as possible. I hope that, at the very minimum, if I cannot effect consensus, then at least the key issues and divergences may be properly aired and exposed.

A second warning concerns a controversial issue within the feminist philosophical community. Some writers hold that there are essential differences between men and women that can be categorized in various ways. For these *essentialists*, the historical problem (i.e., the barrier to equality,) has been not so much the identification of feminine characteristics, as the negative value placed on those characteristics. Barring truly misogynist traits such as empty-headedness, essentialists accept that women are more caring, nurturing, intuitive, sensitive, and so on, and identify the difficulties as lying within a system that denigrates these particular abilities and denies their relevance to power and authority. The problem, then, is not with women's essential nature, but with the socio-political power structure's attitude toward that nature. The *post-essentialists*, on the other hand, have great difficulty with this approach. First, they do not see that there are any characteristics held by men that cannot be held by women, and certainly none which make a moral or political difference. Secondly, any set of characteristics identified as essentially female must, perforce, apply to a particular social, cultural, and economic group of women, and not, as the essentialists would have it, to a conception of "woman" that is prior to concrete differentiation.[19]

The authors discussed in the following sections attack the traditional Critical-Logical reasoning process on the grounds that women (by and large) communicate differently than men, hold different values than men, and prioritize differently than men. There is, however, nothing in my use of their writings which depends on the essentialist nature of their positions. This is because the concern here is with *communicative practices*, and most authors seem willing to accept that, *for whatever reasons*, there are identifiable gender differences in modes of communicating that are generalizable. One caveat to this is that the groups studied and referred to by these authors tend to be, by and large, Western, white and middle-class. There are no grounds, therefore, for supposing that these same communicative differences would apply to all the diverse economic and socio-cultural groups that exist within the world. Moreover, it is quite likely that many males have some or all of the characteristics described as feminine and that many women have some or all characteristics described as masculine. Individual and group socialization, personality, training and personal proclivity are all factors that form the matrix of a given person's communicative logic. Nonetheless, the profile of a communicator as portrayed by the writers to be discussed in the following section identifies a model that will be labeled 'feminist' or 'female.' It should, however, be understood that no stand is being taken here on the truth of essentialism. To the contrary, insofar as coalescent argumentation requires men to incorporate techniques and attitudes identified by the authors to be discussed as feminine, the opposite must be true.

There are two final tasks necessary before going further. The first is an explication of what I mean by "dominant" in the expression "dominant form of reasoning," and the second involves establishing the moral nature of the feminist claim.

What I mean by claiming that the C-L mode of reasoning is the dominant mode is that the C-L mode is to thinking as the *Oxford English Dictionary* is to language. One can, of course, speak as one likes for many purposes, but in formal business, legal, or other situations, one may not. In Canada the *Oxford English Dictionary* is the legal arbiter of English spelling and meaning. When dealing with contracts, constitutions, laws, legal decisions, or academic tracts, one must basically use the official language of the realm. Stray too far, go beyond negotiated national or cultural variations, and it is no longer official English.

Reasoning is similar. There is a dominant and, for all intents and purposes, official way to reason. It is true that there is no one book like the *Oxford English Dictionary* that has legal status, but there is a body of work and continuity of history

---

[19]Code, in her excellent, *What Can She Know* (1991), has a thorough discussion of this issue. See especially chapter 3. Also of interest is Hawkesworth (1987).

crystallized in texts as old as Aristotle or as current as the most recent edition of Copi or Kahane. In the official places, government and business reports, editorials and legal decisions, university seminars and colloquia, it is this mode that must be used. A trial is halted when someone begins to cry. Emotional reactions are excluded from business decisions. Persistent belief in a "defeated" argument is unreasonable. Believing without "concrete" evidence is childish. Facts are what matter, not feelings or intuitions. Evidence provided must meet strict requirements. It is in this sense that the C-L mode of reasoning is dominant and that others are subordinate and kept in their place. That place may be various. It may include the home, large subgroups of the population, informal conversation, different cultures, and so on. The point, however, is that the subordinate mode is not permitted into those realms that involve power, and, in particular, they are largely precluded from influencing key decisions in government, business, and academia. Lakoff (1990) puts it this way, "Men's language is the language of the powerful. It is meant to be direct, clear, succinct, as would be expected of those who need not fear giving offense, who need not worry about the risks of responsibility ... Women's language developed as a way of surviving and even flourishing without control over economic, physical, or social reality" (p. 205). This has resulted in conversational and argumentative moves that are often seen by some scholars as different for the genders. When women's techniques are used, they can easily be stifled by a comment such as, "That's all very interesting, but can we please keep to the facts (or issues or problem or agenda)?" This is what I mean by dominant.

There is nothing, in and of itself, that is morally wrong with declaring a particular mode of reasoning or argument as subordinate to a dominant mode and, therefore, limiting its applicability. In the United States, the exclusion of religious visions, personal insights, or bodily threats from a court of law is a social and political decision based on long historical precedent. In Iran, to cite a different case, religious insight and interpretation play an important role in the courts. The acceptance of one mode of reasoning or proof as better or more reliable is, in the end, a combination of practical, political and moral influences deeply effected by ancient trends in social power and intellectual history. Every society will have a dominant mode, the question is whether it is fair and just given the precepts and ideals of that society. Native Canadians, for example, have been arguing that their justice system should be independent of federal and provincial systems just because the moral values, metaphysical, and political beliefs of their cultures are fundamentally different from that of the dominant group. Consequently, *the kinds of arguments, evidence, and modes of reasoning* brought forward in official contexts that are respected within the culture are radically or substantially different.

Recently, some feminist writers have been arguing that there are substantial and fundamental differences between the modes of reasoning and the social and political interests and requirements of women as opposed to men. The effect of these differences is to put women at a disadvantage politically, economically, and socially. The difficulty is that, unlike native Canadians, separation is not really an option (just as aboriginal women who are concerned with their own status within the larger native Canadian group cannot independently separate). Consequently, *if* the C-L mode of arguing/communicating does oppress or (at least) disadvantage women, then the current debate is a complex moral one, and not merely a call for eclecticism. A group is suffering discrimination and power denial because its natural (or usual or preferred) mode of communication and/or reasoning is not sufficiently mainstream to be easily recognized by the dominant C-L mode.[20] As a result the "official" venues do not make allowance or inclusion for the kind of reasoning and world-view many women require. It is worth remembering that the right to be tried in one's own native language where nuance, vernacular and subtlety can both be used and understood is considered to be of vital importance to minority language groups.

Consequently, the issue as to whether or not female modes of reasoning and patterns of thought ought be included in official contexts is a moral one. It involves the unfair limitation of the power of one group by another. Moreover, that limitation is not based on real need, but rather on perceived differences that themselves are only rendered significant by the lights of the dominant framework itself. As a result, if it can be shown that (1) there are significant differences in reasoning modes between some men and some women, and (2) those womens' modes are generally not respected, permitted, or heard as freely and easily as the dominant men's, then there must be a moral onus on the part of argumentation theorists, especially in their normative role of argument judges and critical thinking teachers, to see that such modes are incorporated into mainstream teaching, research, and consideration.

General Presumptions

I now turn to an examination of the details of the position propounded by the several feminists to be reviewed here. The authors discussed in detail are Carol Gilligan, Deborah Tannen, Karen Warren, and Andrea Nye.

With the exception of Nye, most of the criticisms of the C-L tradition have been fairly mild. After all, their authors have grown up in that tradition and have been trained and inculcated in it. Regardless of gender, one can barely get a PhD in philosophy (or any academic discipline) without having been through the rigors (such as they are) of formal and informal logic. Yet, there is a mounting sense of disquiet, of urging, that concepts important to women are ignored and/or denigrated. These concepts include *connectedness* or *attachment, concern* or *inclusion,* and *agreement* or *consensus.* Although some writers view reliance on these characteristics as *essentially* feminine or as definitive of female-ness, others see them as traits that women embrace or are attached to for straightforwardly socio-historical reasons. Virtually all feminists, however, see the traits as valuable, important, and often trivialized by the male establishment. Code (1991) allowed that, "Many feminists are convinced that traits associated with essential femininity—responsibility, trust, and a finely tuned intuitive capacity—are *epistemically* valuable"

---

[20]The sense of "natural" used here need not refer to essential bilogical attributes, but to such less deterministic factors such as socialization, comfort zones, or inclinations.

(1991, emph. orig.). Regardless of how these characteristics come to be more prevalent in one gender, they recur in the literature with sufficient consistency so as to come to any reader's attention. Moreover, as several have relevance to modes of argumentation and communication, and specifically to coalescent argumentation, their examination provides valuable insights.

Connectedness, the first of the key characteristics to be examined, covers the notion that we are all affected by actions of diverse persons and not just ourselves. What an individual does can have, of course, an impact on himself, but will also have an impact on other persons more or less distant from him. Such actions can include events that have obvious consequences, or trivial events that multiply by virtue of their cumulative effect. An example of the former would be a corporate decision to change working hours that explicitly takes into account the needs of employees tied to daycare routines. The latter might be exemplified by various ecological concerns, such as protecting the biosphere to prevent cancer causing UV rays. In other words, the consequences of a position to a large variety of people are relevant to evaluating the position. The core of the notion, however, is not the truism that our actions have consequences, but rather the attitude that those connected to us are ever present and are considered as a matter of course. The idea is that we exist within a web of connections and attachments, not as separate and autonomous individuals making our own way. Rather than distinct units in competition with each other, there is, if you will, an enormous extended family populating the globe. Gilligan, discussed later, has much to say about this concept.

Simply accepting that one's personal and corporate actions have effects on others is not sufficient to mark a major change in argumentative outlook. In addition, one is required to have *concern* for those to whom one is connected. Where the notion of connectedness determines that an individual's "family" is larger than one might imagine, concern dictates that we care about that family; one cares about those to whom one is connected. This has a dramatic impact, for example, on the notion of relevance. On the C-L model the sphere of relevance of an issue may be much narrower than on a feminist model. What and with whom one is concerned can change as the model is altered.

The C-L model holds a number of presuppositions that are in direct conflict with a feminist approach. The first is that arguments have winners and losers, and, as a corollary, that arguments are, or should be, about claims representing positions, which themselves are true or false. (I do not mean to suggest that every argument actually has a psychological winner and a loser, but that the general outlook is that there is or can be one *even if the parties involved are not themselves aware of it.*) A feminist model, on the other hand, generally is more consensually oriented. That is, the focus is more on finding agreement than on eliminating the opposing position. At the end of an argument the partners to the dispute should not (necessarily) have abandoned one position and adopted the other, but might rather have found a mutual ground to share. Abandoning the idea that argument is a zero-sum game allows for a basis of negotiation not oriented toward simply moving on, but built on a genuine concern for one's partner's needs, wants, attitudes, and beliefs. Argument, on this model, is among persons, not between theories. This attitude puts a premium on understanding *why* a dispute partner holds a given position, insofar as the motivation for maintaining a position can often shed light on the way through an impásse. That is, we cannot always separate what people believe from why, when, and how.

Gilligan's Different Voices

Gilligan (1982) in her landmark book *In a Different Voice* is not specifically concerned with the notion of argument. Rather, her focus is the gross lack of attention paid to the profound differences between the respective world outlooks of the genders, and how such ignorance has had a negative impact on research about and views concerning women. Gilligan allowed that the observations she made apply *generally* to women, but that the distinctions are not absolute. She described her concern as being the separation of distinct "modes of thought," and wants us to understand nothing less than that men and women interpret the world differently (p. 2).[21]

Gilligan introduced two key terms that may be used to encapsulate the essential differences between the genders. These are 'connectedness' and 'separation' (p. 8), and they describe the differences in the way men and women relate to the world and, most especially, its inhabitants. Put simply, women are far more focused on their attachments to others, their place in the web of human relationships, and their connectedness to the people with whom they interact. Men, on the other hand, have independence from others, their status in the hierarchy of individuals, and their separation from control and obligation as paramount loci. One can believe these gender differences result from a male's, as opposed to a female's, need to *separate* himself in order to establish his gender identity, or the immediate inculcation of societal values, or the overweening impact of testosterone and estrogen, or (more likely) a combination of these and yet other factors. One might even believe that they are not gender differences at all, but people differences that merely happen to be more prevalent among the female population within a specific culture. In any case, Gilligan's (1982) terms serve well to capture the distinction, and, insofar as she is talking about ways in which we think and interpret the world, the connection to argumentation is not tenuous but concrete and direct.

---

[21]While Gilligan's (1982) work has received much positive attention and has brought to light numerous hidden sexist presumptions in psychology and sociology, she has been taken to task for not recognizing that her own conclusions apply primarily to the socio-economic groups studied. It is not clear, in other words, if all of her conclusions apply to females and males not in white, Western, middle-class contexts. Her observations, however, are certainly important in understanding communication and argumentation, and may well shed light on other more disparate groups by opening up the idea that the genders often require distinct studies that presume distinct values. This same proviso, that study groups are culturally restricted, applies to Tannen as well. A thorough discussion of this issue is found in *Signs*, 1986, 11:2.

From the different dynamics of separation and attachment in their gender identity formation through the divergence of identity and intimacy that marks their experience in adolescent years, male and female voices typically speak of the importance of different truths, the former of the role of separation as it defines and empowers the self, the latter of the ongoing process of attachment that creates and sustains human community. (p. 156)

One concrete difference in the approach to argumentation can be seen when we examine the ways in which the boys and girls Gilligan studied play. Boys have no compunction about having raging arguments concerning rule violations or judgment calls involving intense, often legalistic argument, shouting, name-calling, accusations, threats, and recriminations. Very importantly, however, the game does not stop, whereas for girls, a quarrel often means the end of the game. Gilligan (1982) interpreted this as meaning that to the girls, the rules are just not as important as the feelings of the players. "Rather than elaborating a system of rules for resolving disputes, girls subordinated the continuation of the game to the continuation of relationships" (p. 10). The connection to argumentation and critical thinking is obvious. When we teach the Critical-Logical Model we are very rule focused. The emphasis is on what is said and how to analyze the words. On the C-L model it is the rules and the words that are paramount, not the partners to the dispute. The feminist model, on the other hand, denies the separability of persons, rules, words, and positions.

Male competitiveness and aggression, long taken as the norm (p. 42), also influences argument to a great degree. As a result, it is only natural that arguments result in a winner, in one person who is best and/or whose theory is best. According to the theorists examined here women's outlook is more web-like than hierarchical. The paradigm is connection: we are all and always connected. In terms of how one proceeds in an argument, the impact is great: "Thus the images of hierarchy and web inform different modes of assertion and response: [for men] the wish to be alone at the top and the consequent fear that others will get too close; [for women] the wish to be at the center of connection and the consequent fear of being too far out on the edge" (p. 62). In other words, aggression and competition are liable to mean that a woman will be isolated and find herself removed or peripheral to the familial and social web through which she views the world. On this female perspective, vanquishing an opponent is liable to involve a separation of the opponent from the victor, thereby entailing a loss of connection. 'Winning' on Gilligan's view, would involve *not* alienating a dispute partner. (See also Tronto, 1987, p. 658). Concern with the *person* with whom one argues, as much if not more than with the ideas presented, will alter one's approach to a dispute. This is an ideology which will speak to every conceivable aspect of argument.

The point to be taken from Gilligan is not just that men are more aggressive than women and, therefore, their *styles* of argument will be different. This is very likely true, even though other factors can heavily influence argument and conversational style (Tannen, 1984). What is even more important than style is *focus*: according to Gilligan, women will be more concerned with the details, dynamics, and effects of the process. Who a partner in a dispute is, what connections and concerns she has, and why the issues are important to her are every bit as vital, if not more so, than the precise representation of premises and conclusions. These things, the actual individual circumstances of the particular case, the feelings of those involved, the effects on others, the motivations become *part of the argument*. On the C-L model, such factors are not necessarily ruled out of court, but they are put to one side as contextual, pragmatic, or emotional aspects not to be confused with the *actual argument*.

Tannen's Genderlect

Tannen (1990) concurs with Gilligan on the essential differences in the way the genders approach communication and, therefore, argument. A man sees himself "as an individual in a hierarchical social order in which he [is] either one-up or one-down. In this world conversations are negotiations in which people try to achieve and maintain the upper hand if they can, and protect themselves from others' attempts to put them down and push them around. Life, then, is a contest, a struggle to preserve independence and avoid failure" (pp. 24–25). Women, on the other hand, see themselves "as an individual in a network of connections. In this world conversations are negotiations for closeness in which people try to seek and give confirmation and support and to reach consensus" (p. 25).

Some of Tannen's (1990) points concern questions of style as, for example, women's tendency to use personal experience (p. 92) or their attention to details (p. 115), both habits many men have difficulty with. Even these points of style, however, stem from the varying outlooks of the genders. For women, personal experience is often more important than abstract considerations that have little to do with real people or real situations. In her defense of Gilligan, Friedman (1987) concurred: "The key issue is the sensitivity and responsiveness to another person's emotional states, individuating differences, specific uniqueness, and whole particularity" (p. 106). Attention to detail, Tannen wrote, "shows caring and creates involvement ... Because women are concerned first and foremost with establishing intimacy, they value the telling of details" (p. 115). In other words, we cannot separate style and substance.

For both women and men there is more going on in a given conversation than the words. But often what goes on is different. For many of the men Tannen and Gilligan studied there is a constant interplay of status. There is a continual flow of meta-messages that determine hierarchy and involve subtle, yet significant conflicts. This is true in ordinary conversation and even more so in argument that is directly conflictual. When talking about problems, for example, women tend to sympathize and recognize the problem as in, "Yes, I know what you mean, a similar thing happened to me." Men, on the other hand, are far more likely to offer a solution as in, "Well, in that case why don't you. ... " Empathy relies on connection and similarity, whereas offering a solution is hierarchical insofar as one has an answer to a problem the original speaker could not solve (Tannen, 1990, pp. 51–52).

Given these distinct core outlooks it is hardly surprising that there are different approaches to conflict. More men than women enjoy a "good argument" (Tannen, p. 150). From early on and in many socio-cultural arenas, women are taught and find it natural to be conflict avoiders, to seek agreement and consensus. For many men, arguing without being committed or as devil's advocate is the intellectual equivalent of schoolyard rough-housing. Just like the tumult of wrestling and tackling, arguing can be very aggressive and apparently antagonistic, but also exhilarating and downright enjoyable to those to whom it is considered play. Given that the great majority of critical reasoning texts have been written by men and/or in the Critical-Logical tradition, it is not surprising that such a high value is placed on the results (if not the joy) of conflict. It is also not surprising that they have as assumptions such separation oriented notions as the Natural Light Theory [NLT] and the convince/persuade distinction. The NLT is separation oriented because it supposes that there is a right and wrong or true and false that is the sort of thing that can be determined in an argument. The convince/persuade distinction, on the other hand, supposes that we can create categories and separate arguments insofar as they do or do not contain elements foreign to logical reasoning. Considered in this light, there is a sense in which the assumptions inherent in the C-L approach are, at core, "masculine." They derive from a long tradition and history, during most of which female input was neither desired or permitted. One last quote from Tannen (1990):

> Oral disputation—from formal debate to the study of formal logic—is inherently adversive. With this in mind, we can see that the inclination of many men to expect discussions and arguments in daily conversations to adhere to rules of logic is a remnant of this tradition. Furthermore, oral performance in self-display … is part of a larger framework in which many men approach life as a contest. (p. 150)

In the end, Tannen urges us to pay attention to "genderlect." It is not so much that one communicative mode must take over, as it is that there has to be room for both. Arguing in "contest-mode" must not be the only legitimate path. Understanding the opposite gender, she claimed, is analogous to understanding a different dialect in a language. If we are to communicate effectively, if we are to understand nuance, meta-messages, context, and truly comprehend the communication, we must enter into the dialect. We must try to understand the customs and engage in the practices as much as possible if we are trying to foster genuine communication. This conclusion is very much in keeping with the concept of attachment. Tannen sought not to exclude or judge, but to explain and integrate. Lakoff (1990) points out that while it is likely not attainable, "The ideal would be for both sexes to move their way of communicating closer to some middle ground" (p. 207). If the genders are to integrate and utilize the separate approaches, understanding is every bit as important as respect. If either are missing, the project is doomed.

Warren and Oppressive Frameworks

Not all writers accept the underlying goodwill supposed by Tannen. In her article, "Critical Thinking and Feminism," Warren (1988) describes the C-L mode and the conceptual framework on which contemporary critical thinking is largely based as "oppressive" (p. 32). A conceptual framework is " ... a set of *basic* beliefs, values, attitudes, and assumptions which explain, shape, and reflect our view of ourselves and our world" (p. 32, emph. orig.). So, the sorts of outlooks and core premises described by Gilligan and Tannen form an important component of a typical male's conceptual framework.[22] Three characteristics typically mark out a framework as oppressive. First, it is "value-hierarchical," that is, it holds that certain things have greater value than other things (e.g., reason over emotion) and that the more valued things are "higher." Secondly, there is a reliance on a strong notion of exclusive disjunction. Something is, for example, right or wrong, emotional or logical, valid or invalid, without much room for negotiation. This is a highly "separation" view as opposed to the alternative, being inclusive and complementary, which is much more "connection" oriented. Finally, an oppressive framework "gives rise to *a logic of domination*" (Warren, 1988, p. 32, emph. orig.). This means that the framework permits one group to view themselves as superior to another group and justifies subordination of that other inferior group.

All science and all human activity takes place within a conceptual framework, ergo, argument and reasoning do as well. Warren argues that the C-L tradition is oppressive insofar as the assumptions on which it is based are essentially male and preclude female concerns and modes of reasoning. What is viewed as important by a given framework, e.g., the definition of 'argument' or the importance of context, involves unquestioned assumptions integral to the framework (ibid., p. 36). Core notions such as the meaning of 'impartiality' can vary dramatically depending on whether one takes an attachment or separation view. For the C-L theorist, being impartial means listening to an argument and judging its worth without undue bias. But Warren (1988) points out that "from a feminist point of view, *impartiality requires inclusiveness*" (p. 39, emph. orig.). That is, being impartial does not mean being fair about which belief is *rejected*; rather, it means incorporating and including as much as possible of other people's views and beliefs.

If Warren is correct, or even partially correct, then the C-L tradition has within it certain assumptions and prerequisites that are inimically intolerant of the reasoning and communicative modes of a large portion of the population.[23] As practically all contemporary C-L theorists personally espouse a liberal view, the idea that the

---

[22]It is worth noting that a conceptual framework is not necessarily an *essential* set of characteristics pertaining to a particular gender.

[23]Even if one supposes that a significant portion of women are comfortable with the C-L mode, there will still be many for whom it is not the main or prime or most significant means of communication. Moreover, added to this group will be (at least) a significant minority of males who share that perspective. Ergo, on any accounting a large portion of the population is left, if not in the cold, then at least in the chill.

framework itself is, on the most generous view, exclusive, and, on the worst, inherently oppressive, is alarming. And, yet, if we consider Gilligan's and Tannen's work it is difficult, if not impossible, not to lend some credence to Warren's claim. The C-L approach simply does not take the values and practices of women into account. It upholds the logicality and linearity that underlies male reasoning and values, while not incorporating the notions of context and inclusiveness that are arguably significant components of female reasoning. Warren (1988) concludes, "It may be that critical thinking *must* be feminist if it is truly to be what it purports to be, namely, reasonable and reflective activity aimed at deciding what to do or believe" (p. 41, emph. orig.).

Nye's History of Logic

The aridity of logic and its distance from real people and real situations is a major theme in Andrea Nye's (1990) controversial history of formal logic, *Words Of Power.* Logic has nothing to do with anything, and the logician works in a contextless, rarefied realm: "He sheds his intentions, fears, humiliations, resentments; all of his natural life is only dead skin that falls away to reveal the hard bone of thought itself. The impulses that drove him to logic, the examples he chooses to illustrate his points, all the contingent transitory dross of his daily life, are irrelevant to his logic, which is what has to be thought, what cannot not be thought, what cannot change or die" (p. 3). But on an attachment ideology, on a feminist model, such a conception of logic does not really make sense: "Logic is a human invention, although logicians may deny it, and it must speak *of* something, speak of ambitions, fears, hopes, disappointments, despairs. Logic must refer to the objects of a common world. Not only must it speak of something, but it must speak *to* someone and thereby institute the relationships in which communication is possible" (p. 4). And, "In my view, there is no one Logic ... , but only men and logics, and the substance of these logics, as of any written or spoken language, are material and historically specific relations between men, between men and women, and between them and objects of human concern" (p. 5).

Nye raises an important question regarding the relationship of logic (and its everyday correlate, Critical-Logical thinking,) and women: To what extent is the problem the inherent unfriendliness of logic to women (if, indeed, that be so,) and to what extent is it the fact of a ruling class laying down the *lingua franca* and then keeping the non-ruling class from familiarity with it? Lakoff concurs with Nye when she argues that the choice of a male mode of communication was made *in order* to exclude women. "No one decides," Lakoff (1990) wrote, "what communication is intrinsically 'logical,' then notices that women don't do it, and therefore rationally determine that women are illogical. It's rather the reverse. The dominant group first notices the ways in which the non dominant differ from themselves ... Then they decide that there must be some principled difference between men and women to explain the discrepancy" (p. 203). Thus, the important point Nye raises in her section on Aristotle concerns the creation of an *official* mode of reasoning that became common in the courts, politics and institutions of power. It is the *exclusion* of alternative modes that creates the inequity, that permits the oppression of those for whom it is not a first or core language. This includes the sorts of edicts made by logic that we all take for granted, e.g., "Only statements that can be true or false form the premises and conclusions of arguments" (Nye, 1990, p. 67). Again, what happens to the person/group/gender/race that does not think or work in those terms? Their statements become inappropriate for logic. And, when "being logical" is the official way to be, it means they are liable to become disenfranchised. When logic is used as a means of silencing, it stops being a thing of rarefied beauty and becomes a tool of oppression. (Vide, for example, Nye's 1990 discussion of Abelard and Heloise (pp. 97–100)).

There are two main things wrong with logic and critical thinking as we know it today. The first and overarching problem is the forced de-contextualization of argument and truth. Nye writes about the difference between 'reading' and 'analyzing.' Reading involves the holistic understanding of a position, approach or story. It attempts to view what is said, argued or told in light of its context, its genesis, its importance to who says it and its significance to whom it is said. When we *read* the emphasis is on understanding; when we *analyze* the emphasis is on judging. Analysis takes us away from the who and the why, "beyond" the words and the feelings, needs and desires to where we can examine the truth in isolation. We can test it for logical truth, inspect it for validity, and then decide if it is worthy of consideration. Only, what is said, what is meant, can be lost in that process. And if Gilligan, Tannen, and other feminist researchers are even partially correct, then when many women speak, their priorities of relevance and importance are very different from men's. For many people, women especially, attempting to understand and evaluate communication that is not situated is unnatural and borders on the meaningless. Nye (1990) "believe[s] that all human communication, including logic, is motivated. I believe that ... people when they speak or write always want something and hope for something with passion and concern, even when part of that passion and concern is to deny it" (p. 174). And again, "words themselves, no matter how cleverly arranged, cannot tell the truth; they must have meaning and to have meaning they must be spoken by someone somewhere on some occasion" (p. 175).

If the first sin of logic was its passion for arid landscapes, the second was its adoption by the ruling male elite as the official mode of reasoning and communication. Had it remained a recondite and isolated academic pursuit it might have escaped unnoticed. But it did not. Logic became the official way to communicate in the presence of men, in the corridors of power, and in the classrooms of philosophers. "In the place of the human community was founded the segregation that logic instituted, between an illogical feminine household charged with the administration of slave labor and reproduction, and a male *polis* with law courts, assemblies, and magistrates in which rational discourse prevailed. Logic reinforced the boundaries of that separation" (p. 178). In other words, the ruling class first determined what it was to be rational, then determined that anyone who was not rational did not have to be heard.

It would be easy to hyperbolise Nye, to analyze and critically dismiss her claims.[24] But it would only be easy if I were to do so relying upon the very assumptions and framework she is criticizing. Nye does not really hold logic responsible for all the sins of history: "Logic cannot be credited with beginning the oppression of slaves, women, under-classes, or subject peoples, or even with playing the major role in maintaining these oppressions" (p. 79). And yet, logic allowed men to ignore women and others because of the way they speak, because they did not take to or know a language that was kept from them. The oppression comes from the exclusion, and those excluded include anyone who cannot comprehend that structure is independent of and far more important than content.

One can respond that this is not true: all attention to structure does is allow us to classify certain highly defined argument forms as reliable (i.e., formally valid,) and others as not. Or, less formally, it allows us to examine arguments in isolation from their context in order to determine their power and separate their persuasibility from their logical content. The promise of critical thinking is great: "Logic will teach you to be critical, to learn not to accept an opinion as true without demanding an argument, it will teach you to defend your position with force. We must learn to think logically, learn to demand support for claims, catch incorrect inferences, search for inconsistency" (p. 181).

And what is wrong, after all, with demanding support for claims? Why should the Critical-Logical tradition apologize for instructing students, *all* students, that opinions require arguments? Because when an approach is official, when it is presented as the only way to proceed, or as the only correct way to proceed, when the bureaucratic establishment in government, business, and academe will brook no deviation, then its power is too great. People are not heard and their communications dismissed because they do not "make sense" according to the C-L mode. They are set aside because they are emotional, fallacious, mystical, based on feelings, argued incoherently or illogically. In this sense it is not women who are illogical, but logic that is illogical, because it is illogical to expect every person and every communication to fit into a specific pattern, be it formal or informal, in order for it to be acceptable.

Argument and Story

In the C-L tradition an argument is generally assumed to be a conclusion and one or more premises. It is an artifact of communication, something that has, allowing for enthymematic characteristics, been uttered. And there certainly is a specialized area that analyzes, dissects, and examines these artifacts as *sui generis* items: they can, for example, be valid or invalid, sound or unsound, fallacious or acceptable.

---

[24]This chapter is based on Gilbert (1995b). In that essay there is a much more detailed and lengthy discussion of the difficulties and shortcomings of Nye's position.

In and of itself, there is nothing wrong with such analytical tools; the difficulties arise as a result of overemphasizing or misunderstanding the role of such formalisms. The first error occurs when the impression is given, explicitly or implicitly, that such an analysis covers *what is essentially going on in an argument*. That is, if the analysis purports to describe the most important aspects of an argument, then it misses too much. Secondly, when the claim is made that 'reasoning' is or should be an exercise constituted by rules that determine acceptable and unacceptable Claim-Reason Complexes [CRCs], and that all other modes of persuasion, dissensual communication, analysis or comprehension are either not reasoning or are somehow inferior, then again, the definition is too restrictive.

Arguments are best considered as interactions taking place in a dissensual framework. Within that framework one is liable to come across CRCs, but they may be the least important aspect of the process. Arguments in this sense can also be construed as stories. Nye, for example, talks about reading as opposed to analyzing. The former takes into account the situation, context, and history of the argument, while the latter attends only to the visible concrete aspects. In other words, the argument is considered with all its connections intact, much as a story must be read with attention given to the characters, setting, and plot. According to Tannen and Gilligan, women use story to communicate because it is holistic and describes and takes for granted the connectedness of those involved. One must know the circumstances to understand. Code (1991) speaks of the importance of novels as locating "moral analyses and deliberations in textured, detailed situations in which a reader can, vicariously, position and reposition herself to understand some of the implications for people's lives of moral decisions, attitudes and actions" (p. 168). Moreover, in the vast period of time when women were excluded from Academe, oral traditions of storytelling and later fiction carried women's philosophical and other observations. Tannen (1990) quoted over 20 selections of fiction to illustrate, describe, and underscore her points. Gilligan (1982) uses both stories told to her and stories elicited from subjects to demarcate the gender differences with which she is concerned. But the C-L tradition denies the relevance of story to the adjudication of an argument. Such ancillary considerations are traditionally ruled out of court before they are even considered.

Changing the emphasis in critical reasoning courses from analysis to understanding, like changing the terminology from conclusion to goal and premise to motivation, would emphasize the contextual nature of argumentation as well as underscore that the desired result is not victory by one party, but agreement between two parties. We can certainly keep classical premiss-conclusion arguments and the precise analytical models that pertain to them, but we do the field and our students a disservice when we pretend that these things are the crucial components of argumentative communication. Moreover, the authors just discussed make a reasonable case for supposing that the style of argument fostered by the C-L tradition is preponderantly male, and that this disparity places an unfair obstacle in the path of those women who feel themselves excluded from the official arenas where one is required to argue 'reasonably.'

Were it not so inherently embedded in our various curricula and textbooks, I would urge, as I did earlier, dropping the term 'critical reasoning' altogether. In its stead, we could use something like, 'considered reasoning,' 'judicious comprehension,' or, 'coalescent argumentation.' In addition to the difficulties discussed in chapter 3, there is also the sense that all *good* reasoning is of the kind that meets the standards of the C-L model. All sound, mature, sophisticated, academic, serious reasoning eschews emotion, intuition, and situation, and concentrates on the real content—the explicit words and essential implicit assumptions that can be identified, isolated, and criticized in the argument *qua* artifact. The assumption is that this particular mode of analysis is what constitutes proper reasoning, and that all other forms of data interpretation and consideration are not proper reasoning. And this is crucial not because this definition excludes other modes from being reasoning, but because reasoning has a total grip on power and by excluding non-C-L modes, those who rely on them are left powerless. It is not so much that logical (formal or informal) relationships must be denied as that other relationships must be affirmed. And that affirmation should bear with it whatever honorifics are required to grant them official status.

Taking Direction

Critical reasoning has been developing on several fronts. More and more fallacies are seen as requiring analysis *in sito*, examples used are framed with circumstances, and there is a growing sensitivity to the need to be less rigid and more flexible. The suggestions drawn from the feminist scholars previously considered above can be seen as a progression or continuation of this line.

The first aim is to foster a form of reasoning that is not wholly linear and dedicated to finding fault in order to win (or, if not to win, then to eliminate the presented argument.) But that does not mean we should focus exclusively on emotions, intuitions, personal history, and situation. Rather, it is the respect of these as tools in the evaluation of an argument and in the discussion of a position. It is the determination of whether an argument involving such information is or is not worthy of a reply. Rational analysis in the C-L tradition is only objectionable insofar as it is taken to be all that is involved in the judicious comprehension of an argument. By this, I mean that the considerations leading to a decision to accept or reject a position, in whole or in part, can and ought involve discussion and information from these "non-logical" or "non-rational" realms. How to go about this in an informed and intelligent way should be the subject matter of the courses we teach on reasoning and argumentation, as well as research by argumentation theorists.

The second aim is the focus on agreement, on consensus, on attachment, on inclusion. This is perhaps the most crucial aspect. For, if we focus on understanding rather then finding fault, then the inclusion of a broader range of information is a natural consequence. This requires a more embracing, less competitive approach to argumentation—one in which it is taken for granted that positions involve many aspects of human behavior, are never simple, and almost always involve some right, some wrong, some good and some bad. As a result, the position must be explored and understood in a comprehensive way as a prelude to finding a basis for consensus.

In subsequent chapters, I present a system of analysis designed to broaden the basis for argument analysis by fostering inclusion and providing a structure that allows for more than C-L sanctioned information and techniques.

Part II

Multi-Modal Argumentation

5

Goals In Argumentation

According to the canons of Informal Logic, the goal of an argument is to persuade one's opposer of the truth of the proffered claim. The argument, therefore, is always about the claim, and all argumentative activities focus on it. However, arguments occurring between people are more than propositionalizable entities whose CRC structure is locatable. They are also communications occurring between two complex entities with a range of desires, needs and goals. It certainly may be the case that persuading one's opposer of the truth of a claim is *a* goal of a given argumentation, but it will rarely, if ever, be the case that it is the *only* goal of an argumentation.[25]

Kinds of Goals

Within Communication Theory the idea of goals is considered to be inherently manifold. That is, every persuasive interaction has more than one goal. On the one hand there is the obvious goal that is the apparent focus of the encounter: It is what an arguer wants to achieve. But, on the other hand, there are goals relating to the relationship between the arguers as well as goals dealing with the maintenance of the interaction itself. These have been called, respectively, *primary* and *influence* goals (Dillard, 1990), *task* or *instrumental* and *face* goals (Tracy & Coupland, 1990), and *instrumental* and *maintenance* goals (B. O'Keefe, 1996). The underlying conception is that communicative interactions in general and arguments in particular are operating on more than one level, and that there is always a balance between achieving one's immediate objective and maintaining a certain kind of relationship between oneself and one's opposer. I shall use the terms *task goals* to indicate the goals forming the immediate strategic object of the encounter, and *face*

---

[25]Examples of arguments in which persuasion is not the goal include devil's advocate arguments, and arguments intentionally undertaken to boost, for example, someone's ego or self-image.

goals to indicate the goals concerning the relationship between the participants, including their need to maintain (or terminate) the interaction.

Task goals and face goals differentiate between kinds of goals based on their objectives. A task goal might be quite clear and simple, for example, gaining an increase on an essay grade, but might also come into conflict with a face goal, for example, maintaining a good relationship with the professor who assigned the grade. The argument will involve both goals, and the arguer will constantly be balancing the needs and dictates of one against the other. Much as when driving a car one has to negotiate between speed, safety, and legal restrictions, someone conducting an argument must negotiate between the strategic objectives of the encounter and both social and relational restrictions.

Both task and face goals are situation specific. The needs and desires of the proponent determine the task goals, and the relationship between the proponent and opponent determine the face goals. Of course, this is not strictly true. For one thing, task goals might meld over into face goals as when the very object of an argument is to impact in one way or another on the relationship. For another, task goals might change as a result of conflict with face goals during the course of the encounter. As a result, it is important not to think of the two goal classifications as being either independent or invariably separable.

There is one other goal category that will be introduced. This is, to borrow from Dillard (1990), the category of *motives*. "Motives," Dillard writes, "are broad and deep-seated determinants of behavior" (p. 72). Motives are the sort of goals that determine task and face goals in a broad general way. They delimit, if you will, the sort of goals one considers and acts upon as well as the sorts of actions one might use to obtain the goals. In the following, the term 'goal' shall be used to refer to both task and face goals unless further specified, and 'motive' shall be used to refer to the more general goals as just indicated.

It should be clear that goals alone are insufficient to predict or delimit actions. A goal G to achieve and end E can be approached in an infinite number of ways. If Harry wants to use Jane's car to do an errand, he could, for example, just take it. However, stealing the car is not even an option considered, let alone acted upon, because Harry has the motive of remaining honest. In addition, the face goal concerning his relationship with Jane would be violated were he to steal her car.[26]

As indicated in chapter 8, understanding an opposer's goals is crucial in coalescent argumentation. In the effort to bring an argument to a mutually agreeable end with both parties content with the outcome, the number of satisfied goals must be maximized on both sides. Let each individual involved in an argument be considered to have the following *ordered* sets of goals. Note that the sets are ordered by a priority relation which ranks them in importance. Thus, Harry's task goal of doing an errand has a lower priority than Harry's motive of being honest and of not offending Jane.

---

[26]In some milieus, of course, taking something without permission is not precluded. Moreoever, it might not even damage or, potentially, wreck the relationship.

The Sets M, T, F, P

A set of motives, $M = <m_1, ..., m_n>$
A set of task goals, $T = <t_1, ..., t_n>$
A set of face goals, $F = <f_1, ..., f_n>$
all of which delimit a set of procedures, $P = <p_1, ..., p_n>$

'Procedures' are intended to cover arguments and argumentative moves such as discussed in chapter 6. So, they will range from particular arguments offered and the way in which those arguments are presented, to non-linquistic communications intended to persuade or otherwise sway an opposer.

Goals, of course, are very complex things. They both direct and limit actions, insofar as one goal might define a strategic objective, but another might restrict the ways in which that objective can be achieved. In addition, it is not uncommon to have goals, even of the same sort, that are in conflict. And tension, if not conflict, is invariably present in goals of different categories. Motives restrict task goals and face goals, and task and face goals limit and constrain each other. To further complicate matters, arguers often have goals that are kept hidden from their opposers and even from themselves, what we might call, following Walton (1989), "dark-side goals." In a negotiation, for example, one might be putting forward one position when the real goal concerns another. Even in a more heuristic argument, it would not be unseemly to present a position as more extreme than it need be in order to provide room for maneuvering.

Goals and Positions

Goals can be hidden from the person who holds them. We can be unknowingly self-destructive or self-defeating. We can be provocative or antagonistic without realizing that we are trying to evoke a particular reaction. We can think we are doing one thing for one reason only to realize later, with or without help, that we were completely wrong. An individual S's set F for example, might contain a goal f_i which will have a negative face impact. This could result from S's being angry at her opposer, but at the same time not realizing that she, in turn, wants to anger her opposer.

All of this creates great complexities when considering the question, What is the goal of an argumentation? If an argument is viewed as a Claim-Reason Complex (CRC), then, presumably, the goal is to have one's opposer accept the claim as part of his or her belief set. But, in any particular argumentation, this may not be the actual goal. The proponent might, for example, actually want the opposer to *not* accept the claim, but to move to another related claim. In addition, a proponent might suddenly have another goal, say a face goal, that intervenes to cause a backing off of the original task goals. In Bavelas et al. (1990), the role of equivocation in a discussion works to avoid conflict between task and face goals. An individual in a socially awkward situation will equivocate rather than offend or lie. One is caught in a snare of conflicting goals. Consequently, it is not possible to state, *simpliciter*, that the goal of an argument is to have the respondent adopt the claim.

The situation is further complicated when we consider that *both* the proponent and respondent have complex goal sets with internal as well as external inconsistencies. Yet, in order to effect an agreement opposers must have a reasonable idea of what each others' golas are. It is unlikely that two arguers can come to an agreement when they do not understand the terms of the disagreement and the objectives of their opposer. In the other chapters, the complexity of positions is discussed at length. Here it is not so much the position, as the goals (including motives) that organize the position that is at issue.

It might be thought that the goal of an argument is simply to determine the truth of the proposition put forth as the claim. Therefore, both the proponent and respondent share the same goal, inquiring into the truth of a matter, and all other goals are subsidiary to that one. To maintain this position, it is not even necessary to deny the existence of face goals, merely to point out that in a *pure inquiry* consideration of face goals are not necessary because the general premiss on which the inquiry itself is based creates sufficient mutuality of task goals that face goals are simply not as important. That is, engaging in argument requires that one is committed to certain limits on behavior and that one's focus is not the relationship between the arguers, but the relationship between the arguers and the claim under investigation.

It is not my purpose here to argue that pure inquiry does not exist. There is nothing in any position put forward here that means that two people cannot conduct an argument where each is completely detached from the outcome, cares exclusively about the truth of the conclusion, and where the relationship between the arguers has no impact on the argument at all. Such arguments may well take place. Moreover, mediators and counsultants put a great deal of time and effort into encouraging and creating situations where arguments of this type are fostered. That they do indicates, first, that pure (or almost pure) inquiry can exist, and second, that it is not easily accomplished. Most of the time when an argument occurs it does so because one of the partners to the dispute cares about the outcome. There is something about the outcome that matters, that makes a difference to that individual. Even when the claim is factual, scientific, or philosophical, there are still many ways and reasons for a proponent to be attached to the result. Ego, career advancement, or the simple fact of the inertia of existing belief all contribute to the complexity of goal sets.

The aim of coalescent argumentation is to bring about an agreement between two arguers based on the conjoining of their positions in as many ways as possible. As discussed in later chapters, this means that a full exploration of the positions must be undertaken in order to determine which aspects of a position are crucial, which are peripheral, and which might be held without due consideration. Clearly, the identification of the goals of the partners to the dispute will play a crucial role in bringing about a mutually satisfactory conclusion. Thought of simplistically, the more goals in each position that can be satisfied, the more likely it is that a coalescent termination can occur. This is simplistic, however, because the *number* of goals satisfied will rarely be a major factor. Insofar as goals are ranked in order of importance, the satisfaction of the top several goals may be vastly more important than the satisfaction of numerous lower ranked goals.

Strategic Goals

Let us consider that each individual S in an argument has a set of goals consisting of each of the sets indicated in Figure 5.1. Let us call S's set of goals Γs. So, in an argument involving two partners, S and T each will have, respectively a set Γ that can be construed as follows.

Goal Sets

$$\Gamma s = \{<m_1, \dots , m_n> , <t_1, \dots , t_n>, \ <f_1, \dots , f_n>\}$$

$$\Gamma t = \{<m_1, \dots , m_m>, <t_1, \dots , t_m>, \ <f_1, \dots , f_m>\}$$

There are questions to consider before going further. The first is whether Γs indicates all of S's actual goals, or only those goals that S knows him or herself to have. In other words, what is the extent to which it can be assumed that S is aware of the goals in Γs? The answer is that since the concern here is with actual argumentative practice, Γs must contain only those goals that either S holds in awareness or would agree are held dispositionally. This is important to coalescent argumentation because part of the process is the participants *bringing into awareness* their own and their partner's goals. Arguers not infrequently lack complete awareness of the goals they have in an argument. The emphasis is often placed on t_1, the first task goal, and other goals are ignored. In the course of a coalescent argumentation the further members of Γs will be brought out and considered. This not only increases their likelihood of satisfaction, but opens the possibilities of the identification of mutually held goals.

Most arguments have one objective that is considered, by at least the protagonist, to be the main or paramount goal of the interaction. This goal will generally be a task goal, and, in particular, the highest ranked task goal. However, it may be that the goal designated as crucial by a participant is a face goal. This goal will be called the *apparent strategic goal* [ASG], or, more simply, the strategic goal. Consider the following example.

Food Shopping   (5.1)

Jim and Richard are arguing about who has done more of the food shopping. Jim insists that he has done far more than Richard. Richard replies that Jim does not mind the chore nearly as much as he, Richard, does. Jim makes one of the following replies:

[A] That doesn't matter. We each do things we don't enjoy. It's your turn now.

[B] I know that; but what will you do in turn if I food shop all the time?

[C] Well, has it occurred to you that asking me nicely instead of pretending you do as much as I do might work better?

With each of Jim's possible replies we can determine a different motive. The argument might be essentially the same, but at this point, Jim's strategic goal leads him in different directions. In [A], the strategic goal is not doing the shopping. It is a task goal, and may very well be t_1 of Γs. In [B], the strategic goal appears to be a face goal with Jim seeking redress for his frequent shopping. Now he does not so much want to avoid shopping as use it as a means of balancing the chores on a broader scale. Finally, in [C], Jim does not want to avoid shopping and does not want any other redress. Rather, he has a motive, m_1, which is to effect an alteration in the way Richard treats him. Now Jim is using the argument to persuade Richard that a motive of his—being up front with people when you want something—should be adopted.

As an argument proceeds one can make judgements concerning the goals of the participants, but caution must be used. It is quite possible that in one would guess wrong in cases [B] and [C]. The apparent strategic goal is somehwat hidden. And, yet, it is important to the process of the argument to uncover the goals. If the argument had gone bad and the goals not been properly identified, then numerous opportunities for agreement might have been missed. When it is known that the strategic goal is [B], for example, then avenues of negotiation immediately open up. In the case of [C], the entire footing of the conversation might change, and it might be pursued on a more personal, emotional or intuitive level.

Uncovering Goals

Given the importance of goals in argumentation and understanding one's own and one's partners goals, it is crucial to examine their role carefully. Two main parameters affect the role goals play in a given interaction between S and T. The first is the degree to which S is aware of her *own* goals, Γs, and the second is the degree to which the respondent T is aware of S's goal set Γs.

In the first instance, the requirement is that the arguer have an awareness of her own goals. This statement might seem odd, but it is not. Often an arguer will be aware of her ASG, but unaware of other less obvious goals. The other goals may belong to the set F of face goals, but can also be in T. The former is simple: One may not realize until circumstances force the issue that certain non-task goals play an important role in the argument. Not arousing anger, maintaining a pleasant demeanor, keeping a respondent on one's "good side," can be as or more important than a given task goal.

It is also the case that task goals can be, in the course of an interaction, re-evaluated or adjusted. Sometimes S can perceive her strategic goal as t_1, but subsequently realize that another goal will also satisfy some other need. Consider a very simple example.

The Car   (5.2)

Susan asks Tom if she can borrow his car. Tom refuses, saying that he needs it himself. Susan argues that she has an important conference 30 miles west of town. Tom says that, as a matter of fact, he is going that way and can drop her off in the morning and pick her up in the afternoon. Susan agrees with thanks.

An analysis of this example shows that Susan went in with the ASG of obtaining the loan of Tom's car. Tom presents Susan with a dis-preferred response to her request. At this point, an arguer can do one of two things: First, she can remain focused on her ASG (t_1), or she can open up her set T of task goals to consider other, secondary goals. One way of considering this is to view the encounter as involving a higher goal, perhaps a motive, m_i, of say, fulfilling her work obligations. When the ASG is blocked, it might be abandoned, but often the motive that led to it is not. That is, S needs a car to get to the meeting. The ASG is the borrowing of T's car. When that is not possible, the motive that dictated the request to borrow a car then becomes the ASG *if the arguer is sophisticated enough to alter goal strategy.*

Similarly, if we turn to the second of the two aforementioned parameters, it becomes obvious that the greater awareness T has of dispute partner S's set Γs, the greater the likelihood that the argument can come to a jointly satisfactory conclusion. If T is 1) aware of S's goals, and 2) sufficiently sophisticated to be able to consider the goal set beyond the ASG, then there is considerably increased likelihood that T will be able to find a coalescent conclusion. Awareness of an opposer's goals permits a dispute partner to find satisfactory outcomes that might be mutually agreeable, and, hence, coalescent. When, in Example 5.2, Tom learns that Susan's broader goal is reaching a specific destination, he is able to suggest a means of satisfaction not previously on the table. In other words, there are goals in each arguer's set that can be satisfied by a given outcome.

Another way to express the role of goals in an argument, especially in a coalescent argument, is that the larger the set $\{\Gamma s \cap \Gamma t\}$, (the intersection of Γs and Γt), the greater the liklihood of a mutually agreeable outcome. But it is imperative at this point to recall that a given set Γi, contains only those goals the proponent I is aware of or would agree she/he holds dispositionally. This means that, in the process of argumentation, one very important task is the drawing out of a respondent's goals in order to increase the likelihood that $\{\Gamma s \cap \Gamma t\}$ will not be empty. When an arguer T increases his awareness of alternates to S's ASG, and, at the same time, opens S up to those same alternates, Γs grows in size. Consequently, the possiblity of $\{\Gamma s \cap \Gamma t\}$ being larger increases as well.

Arguments and Negotiations

One response to this approach is that it makes all arguments negotiations. Treating all arguments as negotiations ignores the role of truth, correctness, and, in moral arenas, such normative factors as justice, rightness, and so on. But this is just wrong. Both parties to a dispute can hold motives and goals that are very similar in which case there is likely to be greater focus on the heuristic aspects of argumentation. The fact that, more often than not, there are (in particular) face goals that interfere with the purity of inquiry does not mean that, even in those cases, determining the truth of a proposition or the value of a solution is not a highly prioritized motive of both parties. The goal of coalescent argumentation is an agreement based on maximally fulfilling the goals and needs of the arguers involved. As the most common form of argument is not pure inquiry but, at best, eristically tinged inquiry, it does not behoove us to be overly concerned with those few instances, however precious they be, of pure heuristic inquiry.

Coalescent argumentation builds on the premiss that arguments are complex social activities that involve human egos seeking to satisfy their intellectual, emotional, physical, and spiritual needs. In the course of seeking the satisfaction of these needs there is conflict and disagreement. This can be over beliefs, the limited availability of resources, or questions of control and power. By becoming aware of the role goals play in argumentation, arguers can better focus on securing their own needs as well as attempting to satisfy those of their opposers. When the satisfaction of needs is maximized, the opportunity for a mutually agreeable conclusion is maximized as well.

6

Multi-Modal Argumentation

It has been argued in previous chapters that the traditional and dominant mode of arguing, the C-L, Critical-Logical mode, is restrictively narrow. When this mode is seen as the only legitimate form of rational argumentation, then there are profound and unreasonable limitations on actual argumentation as performed by real actors, and the limitation of methods favored by one group over another. These limitations provide both descriptive and normative reasons for rejecting the C-L mode as the sole legitimate form of argumentation. In this chapter, three new modes of argumentation, raising the number to four, are introduced. In addition to the classical logical mode (usually and egregiously identified with "the rational"), there are the emotional, visceral (physical), and kisceral (intuitive) modes. This chapter introduces these modes.

The Traditional Assumption

One might have thought that, as a result of the heavy influence of social constuctivist principles on recent work in Argumentation Theory, the final blow to the view that linear rationality is the end and be all of argumentation might have already been dealt. However, with one or two exceptions (notably Willard, 1983, 1989), the social constuctivists have not even fired the opening shot. Consider Kneupper (1981), who says, on the one hand, that "knowledge of physical and social reality is both personal and social" (p. 186) and, on the other, that "different traditions of knowing ... offer differing patterns of inter-referentiality; ... arguments are built upon these patterns" (p. 188). In other words, the patterns of argument may differ from field to field, but the essential patterns are less than wildly variant. It is still the "system of argument" that guides and "argument-as-structure" that delineates human rationality (pp. 188–189).

Most definitions of argument involve instances that are spoken or written by one person in order to effect some difference in another person. (See, for instance, Walton, 1990, p. 411). Certainly, such examples form the most obvious instances of argument. As indicated above the emphasis is invariably on verbal reasoning as the core of the process. Beyond that, nonverbal communication or contextual ramifications tend to be included only insofar as they are linguistically explicable (D. O'Keefe, 1982). The two core assumptions of classical approaches to argument and reasoning are still pervasive. The first is that argument is essentially rational, where the sense of 'rational' is taken as "reasoned" in the Critical-Logical (C-L) sense. The second is that social context, psychological motivation, and other matters that impinge on the argument process are inherently peripheral to the notion of 'argument.' It was the purpose of most of Part One to show that these assumptions need to be loosened.

The problem, for many argumentation scholars, and most especially philosophers, is that once the door is opened to persuasion the entire gamut of human contextuality comes into play, and social scientists, not just logicians (whether formal or informal,) are required to fully unravel dialogic argumentation. Argument must be seen as an interaction utilizing far more than traditional rational means to convince or persuade. In fact, the classical differentiation between those two terms that raises 'convince' to an honorific and 'persuade' to a derogative must be abandoned. Yet, the resistance to melding these two notions, or, at the least, allowing them to overlap is great. For example, recent work in the role of goals in discourse has prompted Dillard (1990) to examine the role of "logicality" in persuasive communications. "Three trained judges" rated various descriptions of interaction for "logicality" which the researchers identified by the criteria of "offering several realistic and compelling reasons" (p. 86), and "the degree to which the source makes use of evidence and reason" (p. 85). Presumably, the balance of the interaction is non-logical, and, at the very least, is seen as separable from the remainder.

Consequently, it should be clear that the two assumptions, the first regarding linearity, and the second regarding the marginalization of nondiscursive forms as rational, are alive and well. And yet, in looking, for example, at Dillard's work, the question must be asked: By whom were the judges trained? In whose sense of rationality? In whose system of logic? And, if persuasion takes place is it because of the logic, or do we do it subsequently, when we want to incorporate said belief into our alethic system? Such questions are paramount for Argumentation Theory insofar as they imply methodological assumptions that are not made explicit in an environment where, more and more, the direct linear tradition is supposedly being abandoned. I quote Willard (1981):

> My ... proposal that argument be viewed as a form of social interaction has proved remarkably uncontroversial; but my arguments that nondiscursive symbolism is a core element of argumentation's subject matter have provoked wide dispute. This is an odd result, since I do not see how one can take the argument-as-interaction notion seriously and still maintain that arguments are exhaustively or uniquely linguistic communications. (p. 191)

Argument occurs between people, and I agree with Willard that people argue in an intricate matrix composed of numerous forms of communicative methods. It is therefore essential that this matrix be examined and, even more, brought to bear as a tool of analysis upon argumentative interaction. In this chapter, and, indeed, the remainder of this book, we abandon the two cited assumptions, extensively criticized above, and suppose that we can extend the sense of rationality to embrace modes of communicating, persuading, convincing, and disputing that are wholly or partially non-logical, but are equally integral to argumentation. Suspending the two aforementioned assumptions entails offering a categorization of argument that goes beyond both the verbal and the rational. Further, if, as argued earlier, we are obligated to treat argument as a *human* endeavor rather than a logical exercise, we must make room therein for those practices used by actual arguers. In doing this, we must try as best we can to separate the normative from the descriptive, and remember at all times that argumentation theorists are largely drawn from a highly logical professional group that values linear reasoning above all other modes of persuasive communication. While this is not to suggest that Western academics do not have emotions or intuitions, rationality, (invariably equated with logicality,) and "being rational" are normally put forward as the correct approach for interpersonal communication especially in formal or dialectical situations.

The trap that lies in wait for argumentation theory is that, at least if we judge by the beliefs one sees ordinary people actually holding, much of the world is not nearly as linearly rational as Western academics. Even in North America, there are millions of people who believe in the supernatural, the extrasensory, and an entire cornucopia of religious, mystical and New Age ontologies. Indeed, it is safe to surmise that far more people believe in spirits, reincarnation, and the like than do not. If, therefore, we are concerned with how people do in fact argue, with what sorts of material, evidence, modes of communication, maneuvres, fallacies, and persuasive devices people *actually do draw upon*, then we must go beyond the linguistic and even beyond the rational, narrowly conceived. To do otherwise is to limit argument, by fiat, to a partial realm of the category of communications that persuade and/or convince. One might, of course, insist that this is exactly what ought be done; strange and inappropriate modes of reasoning or forms of argument have no place in good argument and ought not be encouraged. This, of course, confuses the descriptive and the normative roles of argumentation theory as well as supposing that we are perfectly clear on just what are the canons of good argument. Regardless of one's commitment to the "convince/persuade" duality, it is still important to comprehend the range of argument as used within the world, if only to subsequently assess and normatively categorize. In other words, we first require a taxonomy of actual (or used) arguments before we can decide which are "good" and subsequently begin to proselytize on their behalf.

For the purposes of this discussion the term 'rational,' used to mean reasoned, linear, orderly, is overly narrow and restrictive. This is the sense intended in such admonitions as, "I'm not going to argue with you if you can't argue rationally." But it should be noted that this slogan does *not* state that one is not arguing, rather that one is doing it, from the point of view of the speaker, in an undesirable manner. In other words, being a bad argument entails, at the least, falling into the category of argument. So, if one can fail to argue rationally, this presumably means that there are non-rational arguments even though the speaker does not like them. In this sense of the word, "rational" is often used as an honorific, and more importantly, as a way of negating and/or trivializing modes of argument not in keeping with one arguer's precepts. This sense requires the rational person to think in a certain, generally logical, way and adhere to standards of evidence, deduction and reasoning established by a tradition that is heavily scientific, rationalist, and male-dominated.

At the heart of the rational outlook is the essential role of language, and, more particularly, verbalization. Witness the following statement from van Eemeren & Grootendorst (1983) occurring on the first page of *Speech Acts In Argumentative Discourse*:

> For the elimination of a difference of opinion it is important that the various points of view are stated as clearly as possible. As a rule this means that the persons concerned in the difference of opinion will somehow have to *verbalize* their standpoints. (p. 1)

Is verbalization necessary to settle all differences of opinion? If not necessary, then is it, as van Eemeren and Grootendorst claim, always the best route to resolution?[27] But is clarity of statement always beneficial, or might fuzziness be integral and even desirable in certain sorts of arguments or in arguments between certain sorts of people?[28] Presumably, when involved in intellectual discourse of the sort that occurs in a university (and a large variety of other venues), such an approach is warranted, or, at least, expected. But in at least as many other contexts, devotion to verbalized linearity might be inappropriate or even wrong. I claim that in many situations ego, physicality, and intuition play roles that are integral to the communicative and argumentative situation, and that to slough these off as peripheral or, worse, fallacious, is both unwarranted and neglectful of actual practice. Therefore, the *student* of argumentation must understand, label, and identify the forms of argument being used, and not just those forms approved by the official venues. To do otherwise is to lose sight of the function of Argumentation Theory which, at the very least, is not *exclusively* normative.

Hereafter, the term 'logical' will be used to isolate a sense of 'rational' correlating to the C-L norm of reasoned linearity that ideally occurs in dialectical argumentation. This term is not meant to suggest that the arguments so-called are deductively correct or even intended to model deductive arguments. Rather, it is intended to indicate not merely a respect for orderliness of presentation, but also a subscription to a certain set of beliefs about evidence and sources of information. Arguments, as Toulmin (1958) pointed out, include not only claims and reasons, but evidence and principles of reasoning as well. In expanding the concept of argument beyond the logical we need to include modes of evidence, warrant, backing, and presentation that allow us to identify forms of argument that are actually used, as opposed

---

[27]In conversation (Amsterdam, September 1995), van Eemeren and Grootendorst take the quotation to be a recommendation that ought be adopted by anyone seeking to resolve a dispute.

[28]Clearly arguments can *proceed* nonverbally, (cf. Willard, 1989, p. 96 ff.). The question is whether we *must* be able to verbalize them on demand.

to those that one particular group believes ought be used. In thereby separating the normative and descriptive elements of logicality we cease to condemn when we should be describing.

The Four Modes

I suggest that arguments can be categorized, in whole or part, by not one, but four distinct identifiable modes. These modes are, in addition to the (1) *logical* (in the sense just described), (2) the *emotional*, which relates to the realm of feelings, (3) the *visceral*, which stems from the area of the physical, and (4) the *kisceral* (from the Japanese term *ki* meaning energy), which covers the intuitive and nonsensory arenas.[29] I choose these four categories because argumentation is a subspecies of the more general category of human communication. When people communicate they use, both naturally and consciously, all the tools available to them (Willard, 1989, p. 8). These four categories provide a taxonomy that enables the argumentation scholar to classify according to the mode of communication relied on most heavily. At its most extreme, this view holds that arguments may be given (almost) wholly within one mode and not be at all susceptible to those methods of argument analysis pertaining to other modes. On this interpretation, a kiss, a look, a touch, a feeling, may be an argument, provided it is communicated in a dissensual interaction. A more cautious statement emphasizes the (perhaps realistic) integration of these modes within most communications and uses D. O'Keefe's (1982) terminology, wherein an argument$_1$ is an item offered by an individual arguer within the context of a dialogic argument$_2$ between two arguers. This allows that any argument$_2$ will (possibly) contain arguments$_1$ from various modes, and an argument$_2$ may be analyzed as containing various degrees of several or all four modes. Furthermore, I will argue that to attempt to re-interpret all these to the logical is prejudiced reductionism.

Before continuing, it is important to clarify what is meant by a "mode of argumentation." Let me go about this by first identifying a mode that is familiar to all theorists, namely, the C-L logical mode. An argument that takes its information, for example, warrant, backing, evidence, from traditional rationalist sources, and which, in addition, is or can be put into traditional rationalist form is said to be in the logical mode, realm, or form. Note that 'logical' is not being used in the sense of deductive, but in the sense one has in mind when one says of a thought or argument, "That's logical." Paradigm logical arguments, many of which are not at all deductively correct, are so-called dialectical arguments (cf. van Eemeren & Grootendorst, 1983, 1988.) Though this definition of 'logical' is far from precise, we have no difficulty in understanding, at least in paradigmatic situations, when an

---

[29]I take the liberty of introducing a new term here in order to afford sufficient breadth without at the same time using terminology generally in disrepute. That is, the kisceral covers not only the intuitive but also, for those who indulge, the mystical, religious, supernatural and extrasensory. 'Kisceral' is chosen in order to have a descriptive term that does not carry with it normative baggage, like, for example, 'mystical' or 'extra-sensory'.

argument does or does not belong to the logical realm. In other words, though "belonging to the logical realm" might defy precise definition, it does not preclude our using or applying the classification. A similar sense of 'belonging' applies analogously to the other three modes. That is, when we say of an argument, bit of reasoning, claim, warrant, or what have you, that it is *not* logical, we have little difficulty. All I am saying is that when we do so it is natural to place it in another category: likely one of the remaining three.

An argument, then, may be said to be wholly or partially in a particular mode when its claim, data, warrant, and/or backing is drawn from that particular mode, or if these items are communicated using a form of presentation from a particular mode. The more elements in a particular argument drawn from a particular mode , the deeper entrenched in that mode the argument is. Again, no claim at all is being made for purity of mode, the expectation being that most arguments will have various elements from several modes. Nonetheless, by examining an argument, taken in the broad sense of the term, we can identify cases where one mode as opposed to another seems to be predominant. Consider an example.

John & Mary   (6.1)

> John and Mary are having an argument about their vacation plans. Mary
> is frustrated by John's repeatedly saying of her suggestions, "We can't
> afford that." Finally, with some heat, she says, "It doesn't sound like we
> can afford anything." John's face clouds over; he looks sad and embar-
> rassed. He turns away forlornly, head hanging down.

Is John offering an argument, a response to an argument, or performing any argumentative move? I say that he is, and that it is offered in the emotional mode, *and that to merely reduce it to linguistic terms is to negate both the method and purpose (conscious or not) of the move.* Sometimes, granted, a nonverbal commu-nication can be more or less directly translated into a verbal parallel. A shrug, for instance, may clearly translate to an "I don't know" (although it too might be ambiguous). However, in this example, much more is being communicated, and what is being communicated is highly relevant to the argument considered as a whole. The kind of information presented may defy direct translation, but that does not mean it is not an argumentative move. Indeed, there is nothing that guarantees the transparency of linguistic utterances—we constantly misunderstand and misin-terpret each other—so why should such a demand be made for nonlinguistic expressions? This issue, the translatability of nonverbal communications, is impor-tant. Presumably, if John's communication could be translated into linguistic terms, and related to a claim or a premiss currently in or relevant to the argument, then there would be no quarrel that the communication was indeed an argument. In other words, if we can force the communication into a CRC format, then it is acceptable to call it an argument. Unfortunately, translations of this nature are notoriously difficult. We cannot imagine such a translation without carefully referring to the context of the argument and, perhaps, the personal and social histories of the arguers. But this is exactly the point—we understand the communication as a part of an interactive argument, as a component argument of a larger argumentative context. Any translation we might make for descriptive or discursive purposes will rely on our understanding of the entire argumentative context, and not just on a simple analysis of an individual item.

Alternatively, one might not say that John's move is not an argumentative move, but that it *ought* not be an argumentative move. (Burleson, 1981, might be expected to say this.) But the fact is that Mary must deal with John's upset, that it may well direct her next move, and John's response does provide her with potentially valuable information about both his position and himself. Moreover, if we say that John's show of emotion is fallacious then we recognize it as a component of an argument; insofar as fallacies are incorrect or improper argument moves, they are, *ipso facto*, argument moves.

Wanting to investigate alternate modes, does not imply that there is something wrong with the logical mode. It is a basic, clear, and valuable mode of argumentation vital to academic and commercial enterprise. Given that most argumentation scholars are highly trained in the logical mode and value it above all others, it is hardly surprising that it is preeminent. Most of the arguments one finds in the world, however, do not, in fact, follow a purely logical model, but rather, I suggest, involve various modes at various times.

The Alternate Modes

Having explicated these basic notions and laid out the basal assumption, it is necessary to turn to the specific exemplification of the four modes of argument. To begin with an example that is apparently in the logical mode, and, indeed, follows an identifiable logical pattern is presented.

He's In There   (6.2)

Harry held a finger over his lips to signal for silence. He pointed to the door with his revolver. "He's in there," he said to Jane.

"How can you be sure?" she queried.

"He had to take the left or right door before, and they both lead into that room there."

"O.K., then," Jane replied, "I'm ready when you are."

The reasoning with which Harry reassures Jane is classically logical, and follows fairly closely the pattern known as V-Elimination or Disjunctive Syllogism in a Natural Deduction system. The pattern is as follows:

He's In There—Formalized   (6.3)

A ∨ B, A ⊃ C, B ⊃ C ⊢ C

In Example 6.2, let A be, "he took the right door," B stand for, "he took the left door," and C stand for "he's in that room." Without too much difficulty, we can see the connection between Example 6.2 and Example 6.3. This is helpful in understanding the persuasive force of Harry's argument. Given, as we witnessed, that Jane accepted the three premises, she was persuaded that their man had to be in the room. That, then, is the argument. But, in reality, a great deal more occurred in this argument than its formalization shows. Harry's relation to Jane, his apparent knowledge of their surroundings, her lack of objection or rejoinder, the participants' likely fear and/or tension in being in a dangerous situation all compose significant parts of the interaction. Still, the argument does lend itself to a linear, rational mode of analysis.

A second, less formally exact, but still highly logical example is as follows.

The Bijou   (6.4)

Heather: Let's go over to the Bijou and see that new film.

Zack: Nah, it's almost eight, and it's always packed there by now.

This argument is also straightforwardly logical. Zack inductively draws on experience to conclude that their mutual objective, entrance to the show, would not be accomplished if Heather's suggestion were followed. Even had he stated his argument by simply making a face and pointing to the clock, the argument would still be in the same mode. *In other words, being verbal or nonverbal is not in itself either a necessary or sufficient determination of mode.*

The Emotional Mode

It is now necessary to present examples of arguments in the three alternative modes. These examples purport to show that there are arguments where the sources of information, i.e., warrant and backing, and/or mode of presentation are essentially non-logical, and, at the same time, are still clearly components of the argument. Before presenting them, however, it is important to reiterate that no claim is being made for exclusivity. It is unlikely that any argument is *purely* in one mode, and it is practically certain that any argument can be twisted out of its natural shape and into some arbitrary mode. This said, an example of an argument from the *emotional* mode follows.

I Love You   (6.5)

Jill: But why should I marry you, Jack?

Jack: Because I love you as life itself.

Several points can be made about Example 6.5. First, some will think Jack has a good reason, while others will find it a not very compelling one. Needless to say, the strength of the reason is dependent on its mode: A good emotional reason might be a poor logical or kisceral reason. The argument might also be considered ethymematic. That is, it is not essentially emotional, but merely relies on suppressed or absent premises for its logical standing: "What Jack is *really* saying is that he will be a good husband, and that he is devoted to Jill, and that. ... " And, indeed, Jack may well assent to some such conjunction if presented to him. But the fact that Example 6.5 can be paraphrased into a logical argument does not make it one; it is an emotional one, its force and persuasive power come almost entirely from its emotional aspect. To try and construe it otherwise is to force a square peg into a round hole. Jack's argument, whether considered a good one or not, is perfectly well understood, and in order to understand it we do not reduce it to logical terms. Note that there is here no objection to Jack's having made an argument—there is a clear reason and claim, and in that sense is perfectly logical. However, Jack's reason is *not* logical, its source is an introspection of his emotional state. By being aware of this we are in a better position to analyze and judge the argument.

Consider the next example.

The Grade   (6.6)

Paula is sitting in Professor Tome's office. She is pleading for an 'A' in his logic course. "Don't you see," she explains plaintively, tears in her eyes, "if I don't get an 'A' in your course I won't make medical school, and my life will be ruined. I won't have anything left to live for."

Example 6.6 is an example of a primarily emotional argument. Paula's appeal is essentially based on her *desire* to go to medical school and its emotional importance to her, as opposed to her academic ability to meet the entrance requirements. The reason she provides Professor Tome with is the earnestness of her longing, the strength of her desire: "*If only he understands how important it is to me, surely he will grant my wish.*" Her argument includes as one relatively minor part the words she uses, but also involves the illustration by use of her body and human emotional communication devices just how crucial her grade is to her.

Other examples could bring forth the tantrums of children, the despair of rejected suitors, or the plaints of frustrated spouses. All the same, whatever the reader's paradigmatic case, the point remains: emotional arguments are arguments that rely more or less heavily on the use and expression of emotion. These emotions are often communicated to us without benefit of language, or where language is purely ancillary to the main thrust of the communication. Naturally, there are great questions of degree: Communications will be more or less emotional running from highly or nearly pure emotional states to ones that are hardly emotional at all.

Emotional arguments are central to human disputation. They communicate to us aspects of a dispute partner's world that logical arguments do not. These include such elements as degree of commitment, depth, and extent of feeling, sincerity, and degree of resistance. These are important, nay vital, components in communicating a position. Imagine, if you will, how unconvincing would be the words of someone standing for, say, dean, who explained that she truly wanted the job, but spoke entirely in extremely flat unemotional language. Emotion often tells us what people believe, and, more significantly, that there is more going on behind their words. In many arguments, and especially intimate relationship arguments, emotion can be essential to break a deadlock by bringing attention to one dispute partner's level of involvement. The attempt to reduce these communications to another, perhaps more academically palatable mode, must ignore the fact that what is communicated is far more than the words or even actions used in the communication. That is why we must disdain reductionism: It is like translating poetry from one language to another—some of the sense may well be there, but the very heart of the poem is likely lost.

Two modes of argument have so far been discussed. Logical arguments are based on an appeal to the linear patterns that lead us from one statement or set of statements to a claim. These arguments are linguistic, dialectical and classically identified as serial predications. Emotional arguments demonstrate how we feel about certain claims or aspects of the argumentation procedure, and communicate emotional reactions through a variety of means to a dispute partner. In addition, emotions are sometimes used as warrants or data for claims.

The Visceral Mode

A third category of argumentation stemming from and appealing to conceptually distinct sources is the *visceral*. These arguments are primarily physical and can range from a touch to classical nonverbal communication, i.e., body language, to force. Consider the following.

Shrimp For Dinner   (6.7)

Michael is sautéing some shrimp for the dinner he is making. Deanne asks him if he thinks adding a bit of curry is a good idea. Michael says no.

Deanne goes to the kitchen cupboard and begins searching all around. She seems to gives up, but then gets the stepstool and begins rummaging through the upper shelves of the cupboard. Michael notices, but, busy with his shrimp, does not say anything. After a bit, Deanne climbs down, goes over to Michael, stands very close, and holds out a can of curry. "Are you sure you don't want to add just a little curry powder?" Michael looks from Deanne to the can of powder, and says, "Well, yeah, sure, O.K.."

Deanne was in disagreement with Michael. Her goal was to have curry added to his recipe. She could have argued logically, and verbally explained that adding the powder would in various specific ways enhance the dish, or even that she had a particular yearning for curry. But Deanne chose not to make a verbal appeal. Instead, perhaps embracing the aphorism that actions speak louder than words, she *showed* how important she thought the curry was. Deanne's rummaging through the cupboards, climbing about, and putting a good deal of effort into finding the curry powder was a crucial part of her argument. It was her physical actions that comprised the argument, and comprised them in a way that precludes translation into the linguistic, logical mode. That is, while we can certainly *linguistically describe* the argument (as I just did), it is not the description that convinced Michael to change his mind, but Deanne's behavior. Had Deanne said to Michael, "I really have a yen for curry tonight, won't you please add some," the encounter, while perhaps not the logically most sophisticated argument would certainly be an argument. Even if it were classed as an ad misericordiam on the grounds of Deanne's yearning, its status as an argument would not be disputed. Consequently, the nonverbal analogue should also be so categorized. Every argumentation scholar agrees that linguistic explicitness is not a *necessary* condition of an argument. After all, any argument can be enthymematic. I am merely going one step further in saying that the translation of the argument from verbal to nonverbal does not capture *the argument*, but rather a linguistic analogue or shadow of it.

Consider another example.

Mr. & Ms. Burns   (6.8)

Mr. Burns entered his house and slammed the door behind him. Ms. Burns looked up warily. "Where," Mr. Burns railed, "is the damn newspaper?" Ms. Burns went over to the foyer hat stand where the paper lay as always.

"You seem very tense, dear. Did you have bad day?"

Mr. Burns glared at her. "No," he snarled, "I did not have a bad day, and I am not tense." Ms. Burns watched as he went and fell into his chair. She waited a minute, then came up behind him and began to gently rub his shoulders. At first he tried to flinch her off, but slowly Ms. Burns felt him give way as his muscles relaxed.

"Well," Mr. Burns said after several minutes, "maybe I am a little tense."

Ms. Burns, like Deanne in Example 6.7, decided for various reasons not to have a logical argument with Mr. Burns. She knew well enough that continuing the argument on a verbal level would lead to naught or worse. Nonetheless, it was important to her to persuade him that he was, indeed, tense. Her argument was a directly visceral one, one communicated primarily by physical sensations that, in this case, brought Mr. Burns to an awareness of his own state. Ms. Burns could have argued logically and at some length with Mr. Burns and still not have made any persuasive progress. It was her choice of mode that allowed her to persuade him she was right. This is not to say that a logical argument could not have worked. Ms. Burns might have said, "Don't be silly. Anyone who slams the door, snarls at his wife, and storms about is tense." And, Mr. Burns might have thought it over and concurred, but I believe most of us would agree that Ms. Burns' argument was the more effective.

One might, at this point, agree that Ms. Burns' technique was effective, but at the same time claim that Example 6.8 is not an argument at all. But why not? There was disagreement and there was communication. The communication was used to influence the disagreement. Ms. Burns intended, at least in part, to move Mr. Burns from a position of disagreement to one of agreement. It is clearly an attempt on Ms. Burns' part to get Mr. Burns to see the world from her perspective and admit her insights. In fact, the only reason for denying its status as an argument is that it is not linguistic, and to do that is to beg the entire question. Only by assuming in the first place that all arguments are ultimately linguistic, or even "linguistically explicable" to use D. J. O'Keefe's (1982) expression, can one prove that there are no nonlinguistic arguments.

One more brief example in the visceral mode.

The Window   (6.9)

George is about to reach for the window crank to open the kitchen window.

"Don't touch that!" Anita calls, "it's broken."

George looks at her skeptically, starts to turn the handle, then jumps back as the window comes crashing down at his feet. He looks back at Anita and says, "Hmm, I guess you were right."

In this case, as for example in an argument over who is the faster runner, swiftest swimmer or strongest person, the evidence "speaks for itself," and it does so physically.

The Kisceral

The term *kisceral* derives from the Japanese word 'ki' which signifies energy, life-force, and connectedness. The kisceral is that mode of communication that relies on the intuitive, the imaginative, the religious, the spiritual, and the mystical.

It is a wide category used frequently beyond the halls of academe. And before the category is disdained, it should be understood.

To begin with, we all refer to such phenomena as "hunches," "feelings," even "coincidences." These occurrences are common and ordinary, even, for the rationalist, entirely explicable in ordinary terms. That is fine. The category, kisceral, carries with it no metaphysical, and certainly no spiritual, baggage. It refers to a category of communication recognizable to most people. Going further, making that category into something that is very extraordinary, that includes, say, life regressions or tarot readings, is entirely up to the individual arguer. The researcher, however, should bear two things in mind. First, the category is not empty by even the most positivist standards. Even such mundane occurrences as a married couple's simultaneously thinking and talking about the same thing would suffice to keep the category from being void. Secondly, the argument theorist must be careful not to do metaphysics when studying the modes of argument used. Many people, indeed, most of the world's population, believe the kisceral category is quite full, and that means that communications and, therefore, arguments will stem from it. (Is there not now a crystal store in every large town?) So regardless of one's own thoughts with respect to the legitimacy, correctness, or even existence, of kisceral arguments, they will be encountered because they are used.

It is difficult to create examples of kisceral arguments that are not so outré as to take attention away from the example and to the more general issue of the validity of kisceral communications. The following is as mundane as might be found.

The Offer   (6.10)

Greg looked at Lisa expectantly. "Don't you think we should raise the offer? He didn't seem too pleased with it."

Lisa shook her head, no. "Don't change a thing," she said, "be patient, I just know he'll accept it."

The key to Example 6.10 is Lisa's *feeling,* her unprocessed belief that the offer they made will be accepted. One could explain this phenomenon by appealing to explicit experiences and showing how the process Lisa believes is her intuition is really a series of deductions based on her business experience. Such an explanation might go a long way toward comforting a positivist, but it does nothing to deal with the mode of argument Lisa chose. Regardless of why Lisa actually came to her conclusion, the reason she gives to Greg is kisceral. That is, it relies on a form of nonlogical communication that is a synthesis of experience and insight.

One further quick example:

A Creepy House   (6.11)

"Did you buy that house, Paul?"

"No, I got a really creepy feeling when I was there, and turned it down."

"But it was such a good price!"

"I don't care if they're giving it away. It gave me the creeps."

The kisceral category includes many sources of information that are not respected in the rationalist tradition. The examples just presented above are recognizable and perhaps even sensible to everyone. They have been chosen to avoid red herrings. I certainly do not want to find myself in the position of defending life regressions because I believe there are contexts in which they are crucially used in arguments. Other, less sedate examples, may very well go beyond what is considered rational into such oddities as astrology, Bible quotations, channeling, and so on. It is not the concern of an argumentation theorist to judge the validity of such sources, but rather to understand their use in argumentative interactions. Remember that astrology, according to the press, was accepted as reasonable argumentation at the White House during Ronald Reagan's term. Approving or disapproving of this mode of evidence is a separate issue from examining how the kisceral behaves in argumentative situations.

Modes Are Models

The four categories suggested here form a model of the modes of argumentation most useful for various analyzes of disputes and arguments. By explicitly opening up means of argument that are not logical, we come closer to capturing the richness of everyday disputing. But it is, still and all, a model, and as such is not meant to be taken too literally. One might, for example, cavil at the categories. Perhaps there should be five modes, or seven, or three. But these four categories do cover a huge range of human activity without making the divisions overly or spuriously precise. But, in the end, it is the recognition and acknowledgment of the nonlogical that is crucial if the advantages of a liberal outlook are to be gained. While there will certainly be objections and deviations from the details of the proposals, one should not lose sight of the main point, which is that this particular way of construing argumentation allows us to consider more of the human facets involved in argument. If disputes are, as I believe, invitations to view the world in a certain way, then all the central modes we use for constructing and presenting the world should be grist for the argumentation theorist's mill.

7

Argument Modalities in
Argumentation Theory

The aim of this chapter is to position the argument modalities introduced in the previous chapter into the perspective of contemporary Argumentation Theory. In particular, multi-modal argumentation is examined with an eye to contemporary Informal Logic. It will be argued that while expanding argument modalities broadens the range of this theory beyond, perhaps, the standard interpretation, the addition is not detrimental. Indeed, the extension can be seen as an intriguing addition that maintains the broad integrity of Informal Logic. The argument proceeds by showing that the basal concepts of Informal Logic can allow for the inclusion of the argument modes, and that once included, the normative thrust of the theory can be used to advantage in the analysis of modal arguments.

Informal Logic does not have a core theory that is sufficiently universal to act as a clear test of its ability to incorporate multi-modal argumentation without coming to harm. Nonetheless, the basics of Toulmin's DWC model provides a means for placing the various modalities into perspective. The aim is to demonstrate how Data, Warrant, Claim, or Backing can be uniquely connected to particular modes in ways that make it valuable to consider them so associated while at the same time argumentatively important. We proceed by going through the four main Toulmin categories and illustrate how, in each instance, there are examples of argument modalities that fit the description.

Before proceeding two points must be reiterated. The first is that the descriptive identification of arguments is not the same as the endorsement of said argument as legitimate, valid, non-specious, or (in some sense of the word) trustworthy. To say, for example, that there are arguments that use a warrant found in the kisceral mode is not to endorse that warrant. Rather, the goal is descriptive: we need to recognize them so as to be able to deal with them normatively. The second point, and the major thesis of this chapter, is that multi-modal argumentation does not have as its objective the elimination of Informal Logic or any other tool of argument analysis. Rather, multi-modal argumentation and coalescent argumentation which is built upon it, expand and, to some extent, shift the emphasis of Informal Logic, but in no way compete with or defeat it.

Multi-Modal Backing

Toulmin explains the notion of backing as the store of information on which a field is based. In an argument about law, for example, the statutes, common-law decisions, writings of well known jurisprudes, and (one would imagine) popular *topoi* form the basis upon which warrants are based and data judged. Backings, according to Toulmin, indicate the way evidence must relate to claims: definitionally, probabilistically, or legally are the three examples given, but there is no reason to suppose that this is a limitation. Backings are also the prime ingredients that are *field-dependent*. In defending a warrant or in establishing data, one can appeal to the generally accepted beliefs of a field. Backings are, as it were, the warrant for warrants, except that they are considerably less specific.

The lack of specificity of backing is as it should be. While a warrant is, more often than not, the emthymematically misplaced premiss in a CRC, backing is the looser, less identifiable material that comprises the foundation and identifies the limits of the field. Although there are various problems and difficulties that may arise with Toulmin's backings as definers of fields (cf. Willard, 1983,) these will not be considered here. Rather, for our purposes it is more important to turn Toulmin's notion 90 degrees. Toulmin saw his backings as delineating fields that are intended to be taken as areas of endeavor. In its broadest terms I have no quarrel with this concept. But, as it applies to multi-modal argumentation, it is insufficient. Multi-modal arguments do not delineate areas of endeavor or fields of study, but rather, ways of relating and conceptualizing within fields so understood. In other words, it is not the *difference* between a psychologist and a physicist that is important to multi-modal argumentation, but the *similarity* between a new-age psychologist and a creationist science professor. It is the way of thinking, and its correlate way of arguing, that is of interest. One way to conceive of it is that, if Toulmin fields are vertical divisions of information, then argument modes are horizontal divisions of conceiving.

The logical mode is the basic mode on which Toulmin's theory is based. Backing for the logical mode includes the history of formal logic, the canons of critical reasoning, and the application of fallacy theory. Indeed, what has been previously referred to as the entire C-L tradition forms the backing for the logical mode, and, as this has been just discussed at length, no more shall be said about it here. Instead, we shall turn to the more pressing question: If we understand (more or less) what is the backing for the logical mode, what is the analogous backing for the other three argument modalities?

What we know about emotions comes from various sources. One source is the discipline of psychology. By virtue of research and theorizing, theories of emotion are constructed and compete in the scholarly arena. But, also through the theorizing, academic or popular, we (many of us) come to understand such aspects of emotional interaction as what falls within the bounds of normal and what does not. In our contemporary society it is understood, for example, that it is healthy for both women and men to cry when experiencing grief or extreme emotion. Part of the backing of academic psychology that is available to most people is also the idea that sometimes some of our actions are dictated by psychological forces beyond our control. Another example of how formal disciplines school our approach to the emotions concerns how outside forces can influence our emotional state through stress, chemicals (e.g., caffeine,) and other means. These elements of the backing for the emotional mode are similar to the ways in which fallacies are used by ordinary arguers. There is a sufficient conceptual comprehension to know that attacking a person's character is not a good argument tactic, but not sufficient to analyze the error in depth.

There are other components of the backing for the emotional mode. Stories in the form of literature and, more recently, film and television, provide major contributions to the store of backing for the emotional mode. Most of what is believed about love, to name just one emotion, derives not from academic psychology, but from stories of various sorts.[30] In a similar vein, numerous *topoi* are acquired from parents, teachers, and peers. How one behaves when in love may certainly have biologic factors, but is also mightily influenced by popular culture, personal observation, and interaction within one's contact group.

Consider the variety of ways different cultures relate to emotions. In some cultures showing emotion is considered to be in bad taste or a sign of weakness, whereas in others the opposite is true. Both these norms of behavior and our knowledge of the existence of such differences form components of the backing. The data, to cite an example, for the claim that an individual S is "too emotional" will be very different when S is British, then when S is Italian. It is the backing of the emotional mode that founds this difference. It is important to note that while there may be extreme differences between what is considered "too emotional" across cultures, there is such a line in every culture. This means that if one were to define a fallacy or argumentative error labeled, say, *overemotionalism*, it would be applicable across a broad spectrum of situations. Similarly, the backing of the field of legal argumentation will also differ radically across cultures, but in each case there will be distinctions between legal and illegal, within the law and vigilante, court-approved and not court-approved.

The backing of the emotional mode, just as for the logical, is a matrix of scientific, popular, cultural, and biologic information. It provides warrants, justifies data, and establishes claims. Viewed horizontally as opposed to vertically, like a field, it gives a way of looking at and comprehending the world that is focused on human emotions. To say that the mode has a backing is to say that there is an arena

---

[30]The importance of stories to communication generally and especially to the sharing of information, is one reason why the Pragma-Dialectic school's elimination of "anectdotes" is so alarming. Stories, in almost every culture, are profound and important venues for presenting and amplifying positions.

in which we know and relate to emotions, recognize them, respect them, and, even, accept them as components in arguments. Consider the following example.

Mr. Dorno's Grief   (7.1)

> Mr. Dorno is grief stricken at the loss of his wife. At the reception after her funeral, a relative remarks that she was a very nice woman. The relative begins speaking about her at length, saying nothing but good things. Suddenly, Mr. Dorno explodes. He shouts to the relative that she did not know Ms. Dorno, that she never knew her, and she should not speak of her. Although there is some shock at his outburst, no one chides him. Instead, the offending relative slips away, and Mr. Dorno is told that it is all right, and that of course, the relative did not really know her that well at all.

On the logical level, Mr. Dorno's argument does not work. Anyone who knew Ms. Dorno can make a claim that she was "thus and such" and back it up with evidence and data. But given the backing of the emotional mode, what we know about grief, what it does to someone, and how they are liable to react, the argument is ended at that point. The logical simply does not hold sway. The argument is played out in the emotional mode and a different set of rules, a different set of criteria are relevant. The argument is that no one has the right to speak about her as if they knew her the way Mr. Dorno did, and that warrant, arising from the emotional backing is held to be sufficiently forceful as to forestall further disagreement.

Backing contains within it rules of conduct, procedure and argument. When a different mode of backing is the appropriate one, different rules and different forms of argument are relevant. Note that, in the previous chapter, the question of why Example 6.1 is an argument rather than not was dealt with at some length. Nonetheless, once the connections to Informal Logic have been explained, this issue will be reexamined.[31]

The visceral mode covers a wide range of territory including, but not limited to, physical circumstances, physical events, body language, and other forms of non-verbal communication. The greatest force of the physical comes from the general backing that we believe what we see, and we know "what's going on." This information comes from the same sources as our information about emotions, and, indeed, much of it is inter-related. A feeling of fear may well be grounded in the perception of physical danger, and that danger may be read from physical, but difficult to locate, signals coming from another person. In this regard, the visceral and kisceral often work in combination, as when someone "has a sense" that an individual is angry or threatening. We also learn to read context from the cradle on.

---

[31]The reason for harping on this theme is that the most common criticism of my approach is to say, Well, these things happen in conversation, but why call them arguments? As I have said earlier, and defend in the following section, classing such communicative interactions as arguments is important if Argumentation Theory is to have close connections to, and be meaningful for, real arguers.

Territorial claims, power, and hierarchy relationships, intimacy, and sexual communications are all components of the backing of the visceral mode.

The kisceral mode covers, in its simplest guise, the intuitive realm. This mode can range far and wide over information covering everything from what is beautiful, to what extrasensory experiences are valid, to the justification of nonsensory alethic propositions. Belief in the existence of a god, goddess or deity of some sort is an example of a common kisceral belief. A multitude of other beliefs may be formed on the basis of what might be called "sub-sensory" experiences. That is, they come from sensory computation that is very fast even though complex, and results in an assessment of a situation or event without an *awareness* of cognition. The intuition that event E will (or will not) happen might be computed from a multitude of minuscule sensory clues and simply pop into one's mind. Events such as, for example, Example 6.10, *The Offer*, are in the kisceral mode because, first, they are considered to be intuitions, and, secondly, they cannot be otherwise replicated in anything like their entirety. Other examples, such as sensing that a house that does not "feel right," (see Example 6.11, *A Creepy House*), or that someone is lying, are also in the kisceral mode.

The backing for the kisceral mode comes primarily from the same sources as the emotional and visceral. There is, however, a major difference. The kisceral mode offers options based on field acceptance that is only mildly mirrored in the other modes. By this I mean that one can be more or less religious, mystical, new age, other-wordly, or what have you. Depending on the degree of one's subscription and commitment to such a field, the backing will vary. This is similar to the way in which backings vary in the C-L tradition on Toulmin's model. He cites, in determining, for example, whether or not Harry is a British subject, the usual rules and procedures relevant to British determination of citizenship. One must, therefore, imagine that, as the field changes, so will the criteria. We must assume that a person is innocent until proven guilty, and this forms part of the backing for the justice system in Canada and America, but not for all justice systems. Similarly, as the religious or metaphysical system changes so do the backings taken for granted.

I take this to be largely noncontroversial. That there are belief systems, more or less organized, that hold nonscientific beliefs is not surprising. Furthermore, that these belief systems form backings in a way similar to C-L certified belief systems cannot be denied. The controversy arises not in noting the existence of the backings for the various modes, but in holding first that they support warrants, and secondly that the warrants so supported are components of arguments.

Warrants

Warrants are those things which connect data claims and show how it is that the data support, i.e., warrant, the claim. They are, if you will, what makes the argument an argument when the term is used in the sense of argument₁. Again, I believe that the existence of warrants in the various modes is, by and large, straightforward.

Note that I am here talking about the *existence* of warrants, and not about their legitimacy, acceptability, credibility, or attractiveness to a staunch C-L rationalist. Consider the following example.

Believing   (7.2)

"Cigarettes won't give me cancer," Barry said, "because I don't believe they will."

The claim and data in Example 7.2 are obvious: the claim is, Barry won't get cancer, and the data is that Barry does not believe that he will get cancer from smoking. But the warrant is equally obvious: I will not get cancer if I believe I will not get it. Or, more generally, something bad will not befall me unless I, knowingly or unknowingly, will it. This may, of course, have taken place within the larger context of an argument2 concerning whether or not one ought to smoke. The argument in Example 7.2 might be portrayed as having the structure of a modus ponens.

Believing—Formalized   (7.3)

1. ~[A believes E will befall him]

2. <u>~[A believes E will befall him]</u> $\supset$ [E will befall him]

3. ~[E will befall him]

The warrant is line [2] and is firmly in the kisceral mode being a not uncommon tenet of various new-age and mystical belief systems.[32] Of course, one can argue long and hard about the warrant. Is it true? Is it reliable? Would one who believes in it not take vaccinations? What about looking before crossing the street? All these, and many other questions, can be brought to bear on the warrant. Barry's arguments in favor of [2] may not impress a C-L thinker, but that fact might not trouble Barry at all.

The argument cited in Example 7.3 can, as was seen, be placed into a format that mirrors logically respectable argumentation. Despite whatever concerns one might have of its flaws, it is, nonetheless, what Perelman might call a quasi-logical argument. That is to say, the structure can be seen to mirror the form of a formal argument. Not all arguments in the kisceral mode have this characteristic. Consider another warrant not so easily identified by a C-L thinker.

---

[32]It is also worth noting that the C-L tradition allows a modest version of this in the form of the impact of, say, stress on one's health. It is straightforward to allow that one can "give oneself" a headache. It is also perfectly "rational" to be concerned that one's anxiety about, let us say, not performing well at a conference might be exactly what causes one to do so.

The Wise One   (7.4)

1. "I don't understand," the acolyte said. "How do we know that triadism is the true way to view the universe?"
2. "You have but to look into your deepest soul to find the answer."
3. "But I have looked, O, Wise One, and I find it not."
4. The Wise One smiled knowingly. "Then you have not looked deep enough."

An argument such as this is anathema to a C-L trained scholar. It begs the question by assuming that if the experiment (look into yourself) does not work, then it was not performed properly. There is no way of determining the falsity of the claim in question, because failure to do so is itself evidence of improper introspection. There are two separate issues here for Argumentation Theory. The first is whether or not Example 7.4 is an argument, and the second is whether it is ever an acceptable argument. For now, the question that concerns us is whether or not an argument₁ has taken place. Later we will turn to the issue of its acceptability.

Example 7.4 contains a warrant which might be propositionalized as,

The Wise One - Warrant   (7.5)

To know P you have to have experiences $\{P_1...P_n\}$.

This simply is a warrant; and it's acceptability as a good form of argumentation is independent from its status as a warrant. A warrant takes one from the data to the claim, and Example 7.5 does that. One might argue that Example 7.5 fails because it does not "take one" anywhere. This places the onus for distinguishing between those arguments that work and those that do not on the definition itself, thus begging the question. Saying Example 7.5 does not take one anywhere means that what is and is not a good argument, i.e., an argument that takes one from data to claim, is already decided. Moreover, even if one agrees that Example 7.5 is *not* a good argument, it still does not follow that one is not taken from D to C. It only follows that one is not taken there "well" or legally, much as one can be smuggled into a country. Finally, to say that Example 7.5 is not a warrant is to imply that there are no bad arguments. In other words, the claim that Example 7.4 is not an argument rather than it is a bad argument is to disallow a great deal of the language of argumentation. Certainly, in formal logic there are invalid arguments—and they are arguments. It is also very common to speak of strong arguments, weak arguments, and bad arguments. Consequently, it cannot be enough that Example 7.4 is not a good argument to further say that it is not an argument at all.

The warrant extrapolated from Example 7.4 was propositionalized without too much difficulty. When dealing in the framework of argument₁ this is often not too difficult. Nonetheless, it is important to understand that not all argument components are so translatable, or, at least, not so translatable without doing gross injustice to their sense. The following example contains a warrant that is not so easily propositionalized, and a datum that cannot really be propositionalized at all.

You Really Care   (7.6)

> Carole and Tony have been involved in a shaky relationship for some time. Carole believes that Tony does not really care about the relationship, and does not accept his protestations to the contrary. She informs him one evening that she does not want to see him anymore. When he sees that she is serious, he turns away from her. She turns him back and sees tears in his eyes. "Oh my goodness," Carole says, "you really do care."

The warrant of Tony's argument can be very roughly stated. First though, it is worthwhile to point out that the backing it stands on is something on the order of the classic *topoi*, "Actions speak louder than words." That is, someone can say something, but true feelings are demonstrated by what someone does. Following this line, we might propositionalize the warrant as, say, "We only exhibit deep sadness over something about which we feel strongly." To go even further, we can conditionalize the warrant into good CRC form as, "If one exhibits deep sadness over O, then one feels strongly about O." But the datum of Example 7.6 cannot be so translated; the best we can do in discussing the argument is to *describe* the argument. That is, the event that is the datum, Tony's tearing, can be noted and described, but not propositionalized because it was the actual occurrence, not a description of it or reference to it, that composed the datum that convinced Carole. Using '[[' and ']]' to indicate the description of an event, Example 7.6, becomes the following.

You Really Care—Structure   (7.7)

1. If one exhibits deep sadness over Carole's leaving, then one feels strongly about Carole's leaving.
2. [[*Tony cries as a* result of hearing that Carole is leaving.]]
3. Tony feels strongly about Carole's leaving.

Once again, we must caution that conflating the question of whether or not Example 7.7 is a good argument with whether or not it is an argument at all is a mistake. There may well be objections to Example 7.7 [2] being considered a reliable datum, or about [1] being a trustworthy warrant. Still, in Example 7.6, Carole was persuaded by the datum [2] of Example 7.6 in conjunction with the warrant [1] of Example 7.7. She might be misled, but this is the risk one takes whenever the argument is not deductively valid, let alone when dealing with love.

The R-S-A Test

I take it that it has been shown that the non-logical modes can have backing, warrants, data, and claims in ways isomorphic to logical arguments. While this might be granted reluctantly by a hard-core C-L proponent, I am afraid I want to go further. The second aspect of Informal Logic that can be generalized across distinct programs concerns the normative criteria for determining the quality of the argument. Here we use Johnson & Blair's RSA criteria, relevance, sufficiency, and acceptability, as exemplars of the Informal Logic approach. There may be differences and divergences between various authors, but the RSA tests are usually found, to one degree or another, within each program.

Applying the basal concepts of RSA to argument modalities is not at all difficult. The key is not in the terms themselves, but in the meta-framework in which they operate. Each of the three terms, but most especially sufficiency and acceptability, are delineated not by their internal characteristics, but by the mode in which they operate. In other words, each of the modes can define, for itself, relevance, sufficiency, and acceptability. They only fail for non-logical modes when logicality is taken as the only form of rationality, and, once again that has to beg the question. After all, in Example 7.4, *The Wise One*, the answer is relevant to the question: it answers the query about how we know triadism is true. But *sufficiency* and *acceptability* are more complex; both of these concepts are variable according to a number of different circumstances.

The level of expertise *and* the level of skepticism impact on when an argument is acceptable. The following example lays out five different acceptance levels for five different individuals.

The Sun (7.8)

Claim: One ought be careful of the effects of the sun on one's skin.

1. Alan hears a broadcaster cite Health & Welfare Canada as warning people to protect themselves against ultraviolet rays in order to avoid an increased risk of cancer. As a result of this, he begins using sun block and wearing a hat.
2. Barbara is of a more skeptical bent and requires more. She was only impressed when she read a lengthy warning published in the newspaper. The article described in detail why and how the rays of the sun do damage to the skin and cited specific scientific research.
3. A general practitioner reads research summaries published in a medical magazine in order to counsel his patients, concluding they ought to use sun block.
4. An oncologist studies the original research reports to check their validity before incorporating the results into her research.
5. A dermatological scientist performs original research using accepted epidemiological methods.

Alan, a lay person concerned with his personal health was satisfied by hearing the warning announced on the radio when driving from home to work. One might want to say that simply hearing an announcement on the radio, even if backed up by qualified, relevant, and benign authority is insufficient grounds for adopting a position. It might be sufficient for, say, changing one's route home from work because of a traffic report, but not for changing one's lifestyle from being a beach loving person to assiduously avoiding the sun. After all, it was not so long ago that being sent out into the sun to get nice and brown was an activity pursued by the health conscious. But why not? Surely there is no demand that everyone be so skeptical as to doubt all government notices. There are many circumstances in which accepting the authority of a radio broadcast, even for something quite important, is not only correct but prudential. And Barbara's desire to have more evidence may be a function of her greater attachment to sun bathing than to her general skepticism. We all tend to require more evidence when our resistance to a claim is higher,

In both instances [1] and [2], we would allow that the argument offered was sufficient and acceptable. Ought Alan not have heeded the warning on the radio? Not at all. It was backed up by an appropriate and properly used authority and carried by a reputable station. The argument was adequate to his standards. Yet, at the same time, we do not want to say that Barbara ought necessarily have been persuaded by the radio and not wait for more evidence from the newspaper. In other words, the argument at level [1] was acceptable and sufficient, but not necessarily so.

In [3] and [4], we have instances of professionals coming closer and closer to those with the responsibility for original research. Doctors and oncologists have to do more than listen to the radio because they are responsible for advising many others, and not just for making a personal decision. But it is, in the end, only (by and large) actual dermatological researchers who have done and will be familiar with the raw data and how it was analyzed. So, there is a vast range of what data is considered sufficient and acceptable for the adoption of a claim, and that range is impacted, at least, by the needs, qualifications and personalities of the parties involved. All of the people just listed in Example 7.8 use and require different kinds of information as components of the argument in order to be convinced. At the high end, there is original research and the investigation of same. At the low end, there is reliance on authority, but, presumably not of a fallacious kind.

I take it that what has been shown is the kind of evidence, its amount, and its authority and, shall we say, technicality are highly variable according to the context and the needs of the disputants. Still, one might object, the data in Example 7.8 differ only by *quantity* and not by *quality*. That is, all the evidence is scientific and squarely in the logical mode, going back, as it does, to the original well-founded research. This is true, but only because the field in question as created in the example was founded on a C-L based claim and utilized C-L based data. Structurally, there is no difference if we move to alternate fields involving alternate modalities. In other words, the RSA triad, (there is more than one form of triadism after all,) can be viewed structurally. It is filled in by the mode that is operative at the time, each containing within it its own criteria, experts, and foundational beliefs. In Example 7.4, the guru is an expert, and the acolyte, just like Alan in Example 7.8, does not require a great deal of evidence beyond that provided because they are both believers—the acolyte in the wisdom of the guru, Alan, in the reliability of radio reports of government announcements.

Examining All Arguments

The conclusion is that the techniques of Informal Logic, most notably the identification of the strength of premises, fallacy identification, and general considerations regarding the strength of arguments, can be used in different ways. One way dismisses categories of argument either because of their subject matter or because the various data, warrants, and claims are drawn from suspect regions of human belief and thought. Doing this, as I have argued, puts the modes of argument of numerous fields beyond the range of Informal Logic resulting in their being immune to criticism. The suggestion here is that the techniques ought be imported into these diverse fields, applied to the arguments within that field, and so enable critical inquiry within field-determined bounds. Disagreements about past lives, astrology, imaging, or numerous other unverifiable and non-quantifiable phenomena can and are held all the time. Theological argumentation, for example, is frequently dispute at its very best with careful, critical inquiry conducted into areas of thought that are inherently immune to physical investigation. That has never prevented theologians from dealing with premises, claims, and identifying fallacies and errors.

There are positions, such as that evidenced in Example 7.4, *The Wise One*, that seem to be impervious to defeat. That is, no evidence can be imagined that would be accepted as demonstrating that the position is wrong. This violates Johnson's Principle of Vulnerability (1995) and, using Popper's terminology, identifies the position as dogmatic. This is certainly a difficulty when it comes to arguing against a position. However, it does not carry as much weight when arguing *within* a position. Many arguments from non-theists, for example, operate within the context of the supposition that a god exists and aim to raise various inconsistencies and difficulties inherent in the position. Indeed, arguments concerning fundamental principles, even that of the primacy of critical reason, often rely for their foundations on insights regarding the ultimate nature of belief. Certainly, there are pragmatic arguments on the order of, "Which would you prefer, a medical doctor or a witch doctor?" or, "When you're making a decision, don't you want to consider all the concrete evidence?" But then, on the other hand, there is Pascal's wager, an *argumentum ad ignoratiem*, that has appealed to many over a long period of time.

The examination of arguments that occurs in the non-academic and non-dominant community has much to reveal about the processes arguers use to reason to conclusions. Not all of these processes are in the C-L tradition, and many outrightly defy it. But the person who says, "How can you look at the world and not believe in God?" is offering an argument, and one that she or he finds persuasive. That [[the world]] is itself a component of the argument does not faze the proponent at all. Moreover, it is not the propositional analogue that forms the argument, but a sense of wonder and awe at the complexity, beauty, and, perhaps, awfulness, of existence that comprises the argument. To say that such object-statements are not proper parts of an argument, is not only wrong (bad arguments are still, *ipso facto*, arguments) but it also closes off the possibility of addressing the position via arguments by analogy or other means.

Using Modalities

The definition of "argument" being used here is very broad. But its breadth is designed to include as many arguments as possible as objects of study in order that careful examination can be made. If the guru's remarks in Example 7.4, *The Wise One*, are not considered because they violate some principle or other, then that is an end of it. But, if the position is first explored and comprehended as it is understood by a believer, then there is a greater (if still slight) chance of making progress. Certainly, none can be made by simply declaring that the argument is not an argument.

The advantage to be garnered from examining argumentation in this way is the ability to distinguish between good and bad, effective and ineffective modes in various circumstances. Are there times when one mode is inappropriate? Appealing, for example, to an inner voice as grounds for a grade increase in a logic course would not seem a wise choice of modes. On the other hand, if we recognize, let us say, crying in a dispute as a legitimate visceral or emotional argument, we then open up new possibilities for investigation. Looked at this way, the model may also go some way toward explaining why various communities are unable to communicate. They might be using incommensurable modes while at the same time excluding modes they do not favor. Religious apologists who claim that, "Your intellectual arguments don't faze me because I have faith," rule the problem of evil and other anti-religious considerations out of court. Realizing this may direct the astute arguer to find avenues of argumentation that are acceptable to his or her opposer, and that can, therefore, have a greater impact.

The issue of fallacies of argument becomes more precise on this analysis as well. There certainly has been a vast amount of work done on the logical fallacies. But what might, for example, be a fallacy in one mode may not be a fallacy in another. Special pleading, for example, is generally fallacious in a logical mode, but less often in kisceral where the requirement that one must, say, actually have an experience in order to understand it, makes perfect sense (See Example 7.4). In addition, other less traditional fallacies might be added depending on certain viewpoints. Emotional blackmail, for example, suggests that my ill fortune or unhappiness is your responsibility. By viewing this as an argumentative move we open up the possibility for analyzing those circumstances in which the claim is, if ever, legitimate and those in which it is not. *Ad baculum*, to cite another example, becomes more specifically a visceral fallacy, and yet is open to interpretation as a fallacy in other modes. Indeed, one reason for the current dis-favor of fallacies as analytical tools might well be remedied if they were defined in a way more sensitive to modes. Modes themselves are highly context sensitive, and making fallacies more mode-dependent would, *ipso facto*, make them much more context dependent.

The broadening of the definition of argument in no way means that any particular study or application is not warranted. The ongoing work in Informal Logic is important and integral to any approach to argumentation. I do not seek the limitation of that field, but rather its expansion to include more forms and modes of argument that are actually used in the kinds of disagreement based discussions that form the persuasive events in real actors' lives.

8

Coalescent Argumentation

Understanding that arguments are human interactions that occur between people using a multitude of forms of communication puts us in a position to examine argumentation with an eye to improving it. This chapter presents a theory based on multi-modal argumentation that focuses on determining which elements in a dispute can be used as a basis for commonality as opposed to criticism. It was argued above that the ways and styles of argumentation commonly accepted as rational need to be expanded. This expansion of the limits of argumentation is taken to be descriptive. That is, I believe that the modes detailed above are actually used, and their delineation is taken to be a description of actual argumentative practice. This forms the basis for a normative component, coalescent argumentation, that can be built on it. In this sense, the expansion of Argumentation Theory to include more than the logical has two purposes. First, it allows a study of argument as communication that includes a wider range of actual practice than that identified as correct in critical reasoning textbooks. This wider range gives credence to the human-based nature of argument as opposed to a more limited logic based on an idealized Critical-Logical (C-L) interpretation. By examining the separate modes, identifying their input into a given argumentation, and using that information as a basis, disparate components can be coalesced and used as the basis for a new, more generally agreeable position.

The second purpose is to set the stage for an approach to argument that emphasizes agreement and, more, delimits specific methodologies designed to increase the likelihood of agreement arising between dispute partners. This approach is called *coalescent argumentation*, and we are now in a position to turn to its explication.

Winning

Coalescent Argumentation is a normative ideal. It involves the joining together of two disparate claims through recognition and exploration of opposing positions. By uncovering the crucial connection between a claim and the attitudes, beliefs, feelings, values, and needs to which it is connected, dispute partners are able to identify points of agreement and disagreement. These points can then be utilized to effect coalescence: a joining or merging of divergent positions by forming the basis for a mutual investigation of non-conflictual options that might otherwise have remained unconsidered. This chapter proceeds by defining and discussing *argument, position* and *understanding.* These notions are then brought together to outline the concept of coalescent reasoning.

Classically, and usually, the aim of an argument has been to bring an opposer around to the point of view the proponent is defending.[33] When the opponent abandons his point of view and accepts the proponent's claim into his commitment set, then the argument has been won by the proponent. This kind of winning does not occur frequently. More often, outcomes include a negotiated agreement, a compromise, or a realization that further dispute is futile. In pragma-dialectic terms, sometimes opposers "settle," as opposed to "resolve," a dispute. Even in situations where one's dispute partner does reluctantly admit the contested claim into his or her commitment set there is a strong sense that it may not be very well entrenched. That is, one would not be surprised to find, at the next encounter, that one's opponent has reverted to the previously defeated claim.

Winning, of course, has various senses, some of which may be different from the ones just stated and these senses may perhaps be dependent on the kind of argument undertaken. For example, pure inquiry (or dialectic) has identification of truth as its object; negotiation has the best deal for all concerned as the perfect outcome. Note, however, that in both these cases, agreement is important. Inquiry is only terminated when both parties agree that the answer is the true one, and negotiation when both parties agree to a settlement. Ideally, arguments end with agreement, but practically they do not. Very often, one party is less than convinced, but has simply run out of reasons and can no longer respond in an effective way. In this case the argument may terminate but not with a satisfactory solution.

If one considers what is actually involved in changing someone's mind, then, I believe, this model and its concomitant definition of winning is simplistic. Quine has argued (Quine & Ullian, 1970) that one's set of beliefs are connected in a web-like way, such that altering one belief has considerable impact on surrounding beliefs and potentially on the entire belief set. Beliefs that are central to a web will resist alteration in a way that beliefs peripheral to the web will not. Consequently, different beliefs will demand different levels of certitude prior to acceptance according to their location within a given web of belief. Some beliefs, those that are peripheral to the web, may be changed with relative ease. Others, more central to the individual's ideology will resist easy change and require substantial impact before being altered.

It is important to realize that claims that are structurally the same in a linguistic sense can differ dramatically in the role they play in a belief system. Consider

---

[33]There may well be times when the opposite is true. When playing devil's advocate for a mutually held position, an arguer may well want to lose. Such instances, however, are the exception rather than the rule.

In Paris   (8.1)

Alan saw Barbara in Paris yesterday.

The acceptance of this statement by a casual acquaintance of Barbara's might be fairly simple even though she was unaware that Barbara had left town. On the other hand, a colleague who had no idea that she had gone to France might evince surprise and even ask for an assurance that it was, indeed, Barbara. We ordinarily expect to have some idea of where our colleagues are. Going further, this same claim being presented to Barbara's husband, who was under the impression that she was in Kapuskasing visiting her mother, would require considerable verification. What this shows is that the same claim may require radically different argumentation depending on who is involved. The 'who' matters because different individuals will have vastly different connection to any given proposition. A colleague may be surprised to learn that someone he thought was in town is not, but changing that belief does not, *ceteris paribus,* require a major overhaul of his belief set. On the other hand, before accepting Alan's claim that he sat down and had coffee with Barbara on the Champs Elysee, her husband would almost certainly hold off final acceptance until he had investigated further. The impact on his belief set would be enormous, ergo, the degree of confirmation is considerably higher.

Argument Defined

'Argument' has many definitions. Depending upon that definition, various modes of analysis are relevant or irrelevant and, more or less, important. It is no part of my object to dismiss any useful analytical tool, least of all logic, classical CRC (claim-reason complex) analysis, or more recent tools such as Pragma-Dialectics or Discourse Analysis. The more tools in the argumentation theorist's workshop, the better. Nonetheless, the definition I offer is important in no small regard just because it highlights an aspect of argumentation that has been underplayed.

I will adopt the following definition, considered to be an elaboration (or sophistication) of the one offered earlier: *An argument is any exchange of information centered on an avowed disagreement.* I will not, at this time, expand at length on this definition, but a few remarks are in order. To begin with, a great deal hangs on just how one understands the phrase "exchange of information." First of all, the term 'information' is not used in the same sense that Information Theory uses it; that is, I am talking about *views* and *beliefs* rather than bits and units. Secondly, the more indirectly information so construed can be exchanged, the broader is the sense of argument it isolates. Furthermore, if it is allowed that the exchange can be one-sided, then the range of argumentation is expanded further. A television commercial, for example, involves a one-way impartation of information, so its identification as an argument depends on allowing one-sidedness. Insofar as exchanges normally involve two parties, each of whom receive something and each of whom give something, a commercial would not be an argument. However, if one allows the auditor's reaction (and ultimate concurrence or demurral) as information carrying, then it is an argument.[34] The definition, unless construed inordinately broadly, does preclude at least some of those instances that concerned Burleson (1981). A football game, for example, is not an argument because information is not being exchanged; similarly for fights—they are contests, not arguments. Note, however, that a football game can be an important *item* in an argument if the disagreement concerns which team is better. Indeed, if two people are arguing about which of their teams is best, then the game does become an argument.

Positions

Normally arguments begin with an assertion which is commonly referred to as a claim.[35] Claims, however, should almost never be understood as mere sentences, propositions, or what have you. In fact, *claims are best taken as icons for positions that are actually much richer and deeper*. A claim is merely a linguistic tag or label for something that is considerably more complex. On this model a claim, linguistic or linguistically explicable, is like the tip of an iceberg that shows where the whole object lies. And, like the proverbial iceberg, a great deal more lies beneath the surface. In order to understand a position, one must uncover as much as possible that is attached to the claim. Similarly, to effect persuasion one must impact on the entire position and not just the claim. If the focus is merely on the claim, then the opponent will simply shift ground to a different aspect or part of the position when pushed in one direction. Consequently, the first, and foremost, order of business must be to uncover as much of the position as possible.

Arguments, then, ought to focus on positions rather than claims if they are to proceed to agreement. A position can be defined as follows: *A position is a matrix of beliefs, attitudes, emotions, insights, and values connected to a claim.* It is also important to take into account the high degree of variability with respect to the level of awareness or self-knowledge an individual arguer may have. Sometimes an arguer is quite conversant with all the aspects of his/her claim, while at other times not. One of the most significant aspects of a thorough argument will be the uncovering of these underlying and connected aspects of the position. As they are revealed these "dark-side" items[36] provide insight to both the proponent and opponent as to the extent and nature of the positions under discussion. Dark-side commitments include both positional components known to an arguer and not

---

[34]The disagreement would, per force, be the inclination to purchase another product. Consequently, the commercial would only be an argument to one who was not already a consumer.

[35]Actually, many arguments begin with a question, itself a disguised assertion, that receives a dispreferred response.

[36]Walton (1989) uses the expression "dark-side commitments" to refer to many such items, though I do believe the notion being explicated here is both broader and less propositionally based. Nonetheless, I will use his terminology.

revealed (for either strategic or practical reasons,) as well as components unknown to the arguer as concomitants of the avowed position. This is intended to include a wide range of material from straightforward consistency claims, for example, tension between an anti-abortion and pro-capital punishment stance, to the hidden fears and insecurities an arguer has that make holding a given position seem natural. I am also claiming that the deeper and more intense the disagreement, the more crucial it is to uncover and explore the dark-side positional constituents.

Goals & Coalescence

There are numerous ways to classify arguments. These schemes range from 'valid' and 'invalid' for CRCs, to 'clinical' and 'chaotic' as defined in Table 2.1. Walton (1992), for example, describes a schema that divides arguments into inquiries, persuasion dialogues and negotiations. While all of these systems can be useful in analyzing a particular argumentation, it makes more sense for our purposes to look at the particular occurrence and measure the degree of the relevant aspect for the needs of a particular analysis. One may well question, that is, whether or not a pure inquiry ever exists, or if, as may be more likely, virtually every argument has a persuasion and/or bias component in it. On this view, it is always a question of degree, not of simply being an inquiry dialogue or being a persuasion dialogue. I do not want to deny that a pure inquiry may exist, that is, it is not logically impossible. However, many more arguments may be classed as inquiries if inquiry is considered as a range that permits of a minimal amount of attachment. For this reason the terms 'heuristic' and 'eristic,' introduced in chapter 3 will be used. A given argumentation will vary with respect to the degree of heuristic and eristic content just to the extent that the argumentation is focused on exploration as opposed to persuasion. Thus, two persons arguing a point both of whom are willing to change with relative ease may be said to be engaged in a heuristic exchange, but as the degree of resistance to change increases, so does the eristic element. *Coalescent argumentation is the implementation of methods and techniques that increase the heuristic element and decrease the eristic element while at the same time maintaining a realistic attitude to the essentially goal-oriented nature of most argumentation.*

Since the work of the socioligists Goffman (1959) and, later, Brown and Levinson (1987), it is received opinion that virtually all arguments have two levels of goals. The macro level has as goals the continuation of the interaction and the maintenance of the relationship between the participants. These goals, generally referred to as 'face goals,' are taken to be inherent in every encounter.[37] They involve, at the least, some version of Gricean maxims of cooperation (Grice, 1989),

---

[37]One can, presumably, have negative face goals wherein the object is to harm the other party, and where maintenance of the relationship is ignored or, in, say, the case of a quarrel, temporarily put aside. Consequently, even in arguments where the parties are abusing each other there are still face goals, but they are negative ones.

and, at the most, careful attention to role, status, and power relationships. At the micro level are found task goals which describe the particular desired outcome which was the stimulus for the argumentative encounter in the first place. Thus, to cite a simple example, a student meeting a professor to discuss an essay may have, as a task (or strategic) goal, having a grade raised, while at the same time holding face goals that involve maintaining a working relationship with the professor. (Vide Bavelas, et al., 1990; Craig, 1986).

Task goals can be expanded to include whatever one wants out of an argument that is not in the domain of face goals. Persuading a dean to provide release time for a research project is an obvious task goal. Desiring, for a less obvious example, to determine what motivated General A to attack in force in Battle B by arguing with a colleague is still a task goal: the determination of a fact. Similarly, this applies to playing devil's advocate or even getting a rise out of a friend. Sometimes, the task goals might be almost identical to the face goals. Arguing with a young relative where the goal is to increase her confidence rather than make your own point is a case in which the task goal is in the face domain.[38] *The awareness that both parties in a dispute have goals is an essential ingredient to coalescent argumentation.* That is, it is crucial to determine what a dispute partner wants out of an argumentation in order to allow for the possibility of meeting those goals. This underscores the importance of position exploration insofar as comprehending both that a dispute partner has needs and determining what they are is logically prior to meeting them. The goals will normally be embedded, perhaps deeply, within the dark-side of the position, and a major function of the actual process of argumentation should be the uncovering and determination of the goals and needs of the arguers.

Uncovering the goals of the arguers is the first stage of coalescent argumentation. This answers the question, "why are we arguing?" The goals of *both* the proponent and opponent must be uncovered before this question is properly answered. An argument that is casual for one partner but not for another can be a risky situation. When degrees of attachment are unbalanced and the goals are quite different as, for example, when an argument involves casual exploration for one partner but intense conviction for the other, then the argument is liable to go awry. The following outlines a case in which arguments may commonly go awry.

Affirmative Action   (8.2)

A senior female scholar and a young untenured male scholar argue about affirmative action. When they do the argument seems to be at cross-purposes, with neither understanding or reacting to the position put forward by the other.

Arguing in a detached theoretical way about affirmative action hiring in universities with a young male scholar is liable to be very different than a similar argument

---

[38]One need not believe that every instance is totally separable into one category or another to allow that the distinction is useful.

with a tenured female scholar. The young male scholar may likely have, as part of his goal, maximizing the number of positions for which he is legitimately eligible, whereas the senior female scholar may want to redress the difficulties and prejudicial hurdles she had to overcome. So the answer to the question, "Why are we arguing?" may be decidedly different with various persons involved in the same argument.[39] In order to pursue the argument, the coalescent arguer will first determine the goals of the particular dispute partner and determine where they clash and where they do not with respect to his/her own goals.

Understanding Positions

There are, as just mentioned, many ways to analyze a position. There are, however two difficulties with the vast majority of these methods. The first problem is that, quite often, the reasons presented for a position are not the actual motivating reasons. That is, the proponent puts them forward as reasons for the claim, but they may be more or less accurate with respect to their relation to the actual motivations, beliefs, or feelings of the proponent. They may have more or less direct connections to the task and/or face goals that actually instigate the argumentation. The difficulty, of course, is that without knowing the full position, agreement is nigh on impossible. If I do not know what you want, what you believe, what you feel, then it is difficult, to say the least, for me to satisfy or shift those needs through argumentation.

The second difficulty is that most analytical tools focus on the desire of the respondent to eliminate, defeat or otherwise invalidate the proponent's reasons. Although this can be important in certain circumstances, it should not be the major goal of a respondent, and certainly not at the outset of a dispute. *If we take seriously the idea that claims are icons for positions that connect to a myriad of other beliefs and assorted psycho-social elements, then uncovering those items becomes a precursor to successful argumentative communication.* On this model, understanding a position is a prerequisite for further pursuit of the argumentation.

Understanding a position clearly involves far more than knowing a claim and its immediate supporting reasons. Rather, understanding a position involves knowing why someone would hold that particular position and how someone who holds that position would think and feel. This means one must garner not only the facts that support the claim, but the values, emotions and attitudes that go along with the outlook attached to the claim. Indeed, the deeper the disagreement, the more essential is the view that the claim represents a position. One cannot be said to properly understand a position unless one can comprehend all that the position entails, and can, at least theoretically, put oneself in the place of a holder of that position. But putting oneself in the place of a dispute partner necessarily goes well

---

[39] Actually, on this schema the notion of "the same argument" really does not make sense. Arguments will be *essentially* different when taking place between different people.

beyond adopting the propositional component identified as the claim. It includes taking on the world view, adopting the attitudes and values, the very psychic mantle of one's dispute partner. This is not an easy undertaking, as it involves revealing a position as opposed to simply hearing a claim.

Uncovering a position, as opposed to attacking a claim, is a much more difficult and involved procedure. For one thing, many proponents who are questioned about a claim have not created an articulatable position to accompany it. Rather, there is a loosely connected set of beliefs, facts, insights, and attitudes that are brought forth as the argumentation demands. Ergo, any particular commitment may be withdrawn, altered, or contradicted without the proponent even noticing, let alone making allowance. But such moves, rather than being victories for the respondent, can better be viewed as signposts for the unraveling of the actual position being held by the proponent. This is, of course, not always the case. Sometimes a proponent's position is fully articulated and understood by him or herself. A holder of a particular political or social view, say conservative politics or anti-abortion, may have a great deal of the position laid out and prepared. Similarly, a scholar who strongly believes in mind–body dualism may be able to present a case that includes a good deal beyond simple claims and reasons. Even in these cases, I would maintain, the vagaries of the actual processing of the dispute in this particular circumstance are liable to fog the aspects of the position important to the respondent at that time. Furthermore, there may always be (even fundamental) aspects of the position that still remain to be uncovered and revealed to both parties.

Coalescence and Alternate Modalities

Understanding a position requires exploration of all the available modes of argumentation. These include, as previously argued, the logical, emotional, visceral, and kisceral (or intuitive) aspects of a view. Arguers' beliefs and attitudes derive from a wide range of sources, only one of which is the logical. In order to go beyond the simple examination of a claim to the comprehension of a full position, the connections with these other modes needs be explored. In order to clarify this requirement, Example 8.2, which concerns a young male job seeker and a tenured female scholar, is used to very briefly examine each of the four categories.

The *logical* realm is, in many ways, the simplest. It would include moral and practical arguments for affirmative action, and involve an exploration of the reasons for them, their consistency with respect to related positions, and the cogency of reasons in support. The emphasis is on verbal exploration and, perhaps, the presentation and discussion of numerous CRCs. The emotional level, however, is a different matter. Here different arguers, even if they hold the same or similar logical positions, are liable to diverge dramatically. The young male job seeker may be arguing from a base of fear for his future and his ability to pursue his desired career. Understanding that his view is based, at least in part, on his fears for his future security and happiness is crucial to understanding his position. One cannot, for example, expect him to argue casually or be patient and non-reactive in the face of cavalier arguments. The senior female scholar, on the other hand, may be nursing considerable anger over the extreme difficulties she herself faced in arriving at her present position. She might feel that opposition to affirmative action is, *ipso facto*, a signal of sexism that ignores the great injustices that have been perpetrated upon her sex. Each of these two arguers will have a radically different emotional base for their argumentation, and understanding the position will involve uncovering—explicitly or implicitly—their respective emotional cores.

In this example, the visceral includes the female scholar's secure position as tenured and the young scholar's status of (perhaps relative) unemployment. These social and economic factors are inherent in the likely bias that will invariably be attached to the positions.[40] People, for example, who are oppressed and hungry will listen to arguments that others will not. The *kisceral* mode enters as well. The young scholar may believe that he is "perfect" for a job limited to women, and "be sure" that he would have gotten it otherwise. This hunch might well be a major factor in his position and impact greatly on his degree of attachment to it. The senior female scholar, on the other hand, may have a strong vision, an almost palpable insight, into a world in which sex is irrelevant to scholarly appointment, and where men and women interact in academe without regard for sex or gender.

Table 8.1 below exemplifies the information that can (and should be) garnered in the course of a dispute *for each partner*.

The itemization of the complexity of each partner's position enables arguers to separate those points on which there is agreement. This will be valuable in the third stage when coalescence is attempted. This second stage of argument, the exploration of the participants' positions, is only complete when all of this is open and understood. Conceivably, this may never happen perfectly. In fact, given the extraordinarily complex nature of positions, it is tempting to say that full awareness of another's position never does happen completely. Still, the second stage answers the question, "What are we arguing about?" and the degree to which coalescence is liable to be attained is a function of the degree to which that question is answered.

TABLE 8.1
Position Analysis

Logical	*Emotional*	*Visceral*	*Kisceral*
beliefs	attitudes	situation	intuition
CRCs	feelings	socio-eco context	insights
reasons	emotions	physicality	hunches

---

[40]I am not, of course, maintaining that every young male scholar is against affirmative action, or conversely for senior female scholars. These positions are presented as an example only.

Sine Qua Non

Real arguments are those that involve a conflict between arguers' needs, goals, ideas, and outlooks. Although argument can be a relatively idle exploration of a subject matter or a detached inquiry into the truth of a matter, most are not. Most arguments involve, at the least, a combination of task goals and the correction or alteration of received dis-preferred responses. The natural impulse in such situations is to attack and criticize the presented claim and/or data and warrants with the goal of defeating the stated position, thus leaving the respondent with no choice but to accept the alternative position put forward by the dispute partner. Acceding to such impulses ignores the first two stages of coalescent argumentation, namely, identification of goals and exploration of positions. It is, therefore, likely to lead to increased conflict or even acrimony, and misdirect opportunities for agreement. The end result, insofar as the process is focused on 'winning,' is liable to be unsatisfactory for both parties, and end in disagreement or, at best, reluctant compliance.[41]

It is, perhaps, not too strong to say that the most crucial element in coalescent argumentation is empathy. Indeed, the greater the disagreement, the further apart the initial stances of the dispute partners, the more important (and the more difficult) is the requirement for empathy. And here the avowed normative nature of this project is no more apparent. *Empathy* is an attitude and an act of will. It requires paying attention to the entire range of communicative and epistemic modes available in order to project oneself into another's position. Speaking of the role of emotion in argument, Walton says that in order to "find premises that represent real commitments the respondent will stick to and not retract easily, the arguer must judge *by empathy* what the respondent's basic position is" (Walton, 1992, p. 108, emphasis added). While here it is argued that emotion is but one of the non-logical avenues that must be explored, the role of empathy is at least as important. One does not become empathetic without wanting to. The quality of listening and observation required for the empathic comprehension of another's position is no mean feat; it demands, at least temporarily, the suspension of the drive to persuade or convince, i.e., to win, in favor of the desire to agree. The third stage of coalescent argumentation, the attempt to find points of coalescence, requires empathy.

Coalescence involves the merging of two things into one. According to the *Oxford English Dictionary* (1972), to *coalesce*, in the relevant sense, means, "To unite or come together, so as to form one" (p.448). In an actual argumentation, coalescence will be a matter of degree. It is unrealistic to expect two diverse positions to completely meld into one, and that is neither the point nor the claim of coalescent argumentation. Rather, the goal is to locate those points of belief and/or attitude that are held in common by the conflictual positions. Beginning with these points of agreement, one can then work down toward areas where disagreement lies. By focusing on agreement, the third stage, the stage of coalescence, aids in

---

[41]There are no doubt times when reluctant compliance is quite satisfactory. When returning a toaster one day past warranty, one may be quite happy with such an outcome. More often, however, long term face-goal considerations are relevant.

answering the question, "How can we come to agreement?" Or, focusing on the positions, "How can our positions accommodate each other?" The key is the empathic awareness that certain beliefs, attitudes, situations, and intuitions are held in common by the dispute partners. With the positions clear and understood in the sense described above there should exist some common understanding of each position, why it is held, what it means to the holder, the importance of the position in the holder's world view, and what sorts of needs the position fulfills. The move toward coalescence involves attempting to respect and, therefore, accommodate as much as possible the needs, desires, beliefs, and attitudes of both participants.

Merging Positions

Once a position has been understood, ideally (but not necessarily) by each side comprehending the other side's position, then the argument can proceed to the coalescent stage. The goal of the coalescent stage is to merge the two positions as much as possible, thereby creating opportunities for investigating further options. The initial focus, then, is on points or attitudes the positions share rather than those that are separately held. The emphasis, if you will, is on convergence as opposed to divergence. In this way, the shared goals, values, and attitudes held by both participants, form the starting point for further discussion. The key is the notion that positions are most often improperly understood, frequently as much by the proponent as by the opponent. Moreover, divergences often occur at points in the argument well beyond the initial assumptions and attitudes from which the disputed claim(s) flow. A couple arguing about the best school for their child will both share beliefs, let us suppose, about the importance of education and of finding the right school. By beginning with these common grounds, the argument can come to focus on, for example, what each parent views as central to good education and the special needs of this particular child. Similarly, heads of state negotiating nonaggression agreements may begin with their desire to provide peace for their populations and alleviate their respective economies from the burden of defense costs. In the context of these agreements, the differences that appear are more amenable to conciliation, negotiation, and exploration.

It is impossible to state unequivocally that any two opposed positions share some common points. Nonetheless, the vast majority of arguments that occur most of the time in most of our lives are had with people whose *weltanschauungun* are not *wholly* foreign to our own.[42] In arguing about schools, we both believe in the

---

[42]There is an overwhelming inclination, when faced with statements such as these, for a reader to immediately begin to catalogue numerous arguments that, in fact, involve no position overlap at all. One might, perhaps, think of a fundamentalist Christian and a humanist radical feminist arguing about abortion or lesbian rights. In such cases, it may well be that the shared aspects are so minimal as to be argumentatively useless or even nonexistent. Such cases no doubt exist, but they do not represent the sort of arguments most of us find ourselves in most of the time. And, they especially do not represent the arguments that we truly hope or want to resolve on an interpersonal basis.

importance of education. In arguing about civilian control of the police, we both believe policing is necessary and crime must be controlled. Furthermore, when a respondent *understands* a proponent's fear of crime, his feeling of alarm regarding his own safety and that of his family, then the exercise ceases to be an intellectual one and transforms itself into an issue with which both parties can empathize.

Even when all else fails, coalescent argumentation, at the least, holds open the likelihood of deepened insights into the conflicting positions, thereby shedding light on the deeper roots of the disagreement. In this regard, the adage "we agreed to disagree," is not without relevance. It indicates an awareness of differences that cannot, at least at that time, be resolved. However, what is crucial is the awareness that such differences may well not be central to the disagreement and, therefore, not stand in the way of continued progress in the argument. That is, by taking a coalescent attitude, we might agree to disagree on matter P, while continuing to discuss ways of resolving Q and R. Since the focus is on what is common between the positions, the significance of what is divergent diminishes. The question becomes, is our difference concerning P so central that it cannot be isolated, worked around, or otherwise be taken into account? In this sense, agreeing to disagree does not preclude further agreement; rather, it changes the direction of the discussion so that it can go around the contentious issue and focus on other matters.

Arguments normally commence with disagreement. A claim is uttered and opposition is voiced in response. The resolution may come quite quickly if the disagreement is a minor one or, say, a mere matter of correcting misinformation. If, on the other hand, the matter appears to resist simple resolution, then a more thorough resolution process is necessary. At this point, rigorous position examination is required, and the effort to find points of agreement should commence. It is essential, moreover, that such exploration occur on all levels of communication and not merely on the logical. Table 8.2 illustrates this process.

As with any model, the separations indicated in Table 8.2 are not likely to fall into neat little boxes. Intuitions, emotions, and beliefs often interact to form an inextricable matrix that is the position. Nonetheless, the chart helps to emphasize

TABLE 8.2
Levels of Argumentation

Level	Item, e.g.	Logical	Emotional	Visceral	Kisceral
L	Claim	Belief P	Attitude P	Attitude Π	Situation π
L - 1	Data	Belief $Q{\rightarrow}P$	Att. P & Q	Sit. $\Pi + \Theta$	Int. $\pi + \Theta$
L - 2	Backing	Assumptions $R_1,...,R_n$	Feelings $R1,...,R_n$	Predictions $\Omega_1,...,\Omega_n$	Insights $\omega_1,...,\omega_n$
...	...	...	...	...	...
L - n	Basic Outlook	Foundational Beliefs	Deep Feelings	Life History, Expectations	Ultimate Convictions

that the various modalities all require exploration. The basis of the disagreement may not really be on the logical level, but might be focused on various intuitions which themselves support certain beliefs. Alternatively, the most aggravated source of dissension might be in the visceral mode, where one participant's personal history or current situation creates blocks to alteration of the position. By separating these items the possibility of working around a key disagreement is increased. In other words, a crucial and tightly held belief or deeply ingrained attitude might be bypassed by steering agreement toward items that are not in conflict or where there is, at least, the possibility of movement. For example, a smoker who holds dearly the kisceral intuition that she will not be harmed by cigarette smoking if she does not believe it will harm her, might be persuaded by an appeal to another mode that involves the potential harm to others who do not share her surety.

Exploring for Agreement

Examination of Table 8.2 reveals several specific ways in which agreement can be explored. The first is by moving deeper and deeper into the positions in an effort to find points of presumption or outlook that are shared. This vertical inquiry involves examination of more fundamental beliefs and attitudes on which the position rests. Frequently, moving further back into the position may permit arguers to agree that the more surface consequences are not necessary concomitants or consequences of the lower items. This enables discussion of why particular conse- quential paths are chosen rather than others, and can de-stabilize the belief that, say, attitude R_j is necessarily connected to attitude P. In other words, one might be able to effect movement on P while not undermining R_j, but rather by showing that the feeling R_j is not inconsistent with the feeling that $\sim P$.

A second way would be to take a horizontal approach. In this instance, the argument moves from one mode to another for one of several reasons. In the first instance, the opponent might become aware that the proponent's logical beliefs are not sufficiently coherent to be gainfully explored. This would indicate that the true grounding of the position is to be found in a different mode. Resistance on the emotional level, for example, might be dealt with by an analysis on the logical level. This is the approach taken in rational-emotive therapy where strong feelings and fears are explored through logical analysis until their attitudinal nature must be directly confronted. Even where the realization that a particular mode is active does not aid in moving the argument further, the information garnered thereby can be valuable. In other words, one might not alter a strong kisceral intuition, such as the belief in a higher spiritual being, but, as a result of isolating the kisceral aspect, it may be incorporated into the argument in a more helpful way; or, alternatively, it can be identified and explored for the purpose of bracketing or earmarking as a key assumption.

Finally, there may be a diagonal approach wherein it is realized or suspected that the dispute partners are operating in different modes. This can result in arguing at cross-purposes. If one dispute partner is talking about feelings and the other about beliefs, they may not be registering each other's essential position. The awareness that a dispute partner is "coming from a different place," can lead an opponent to change ground in an effort to better explore the presented position. Alan might, for example, be touting a particular film as the choice for the evening on the basis of its reviews and cinematic qualities, whereas Barbara is opposing its choice as a result of her particular mood that evening. The realization that different modes are operating means that while Alan might be wasting his time continuing the logical argumentation, he might get further by dealing directly with Barbara's mood. Barbara, on the other hand, can greatly simplify matters by agreeing with Alan that the movie received the plaudits he claims for it, and, perhaps if she were feeling differently, she might be inclined to see it. Alan is more likely to understand when he sees the basis of her opposition in the correct light.

Since positions are a matrix built of items from (normally) all four modes, the knowledge that one is central or dominant in a particular dispute can be crucial. Consider, as an example, a discussion concerning legislation intended to limit cigarette smoking. There might be radically different grounds for opposition to its abandonment depending on which mode is operative. Seeking agreement on its evils will be greatly facilitated by identifying the correct mode. A member of the tobacco industry, for example, might well have a logically based position that relies heavily on denying the legitimacy of the scientific evidence. On the other hand, a confirmed smoker might rest his refusal to quit on the attitude that he does not care about the consequences, and is willing to risk future illness for present satisfaction. This emotional argument makes questions about the veracity of the empirical evidence irrelevant. Viscerally, someone whose livelihood depends on cigarette sales, say the owner of a small corner store, might oppose the regulations on the grounds they would devastate his business. Finally, a cigarette smoker might claim that she has the kisceral intuition that no harm will befall her if she herself does not believe it will. In each case, there may be opportunities for agreement in the other areas which, if settled on and isolated, can better focus on the key areas of disagreement and potentially lead to compromises and the satisfaction of mutual task goals.

Real Argumentation

The reasons we present for positions are often only loosely related to the actual motivations, attitudes, and drives that lead us to it. These reasons, veridical or otherwise, provide an initial basis for the commencement of argumentation. But the process of argumentation may well lead us away from them as they are seen to be less compelling than required for the adoption of the relevant claim. The exploration of the position on which the claim rests can open up areas of communication where agreement may be established. As this occurs, the ground for alternative solutions to problems, various negotiated conclusions, and bracketing of (possibly important) commitments that are not central to the disagreement is more likely. In coalescent argumentation the exchange of information is central to the goal of agreement. By using the information garnered to understand the position an agreement can be formulated that is satisfactory to both parties.

Naturally, no claim whatever is being made that agreement will be the inevitable result of argumentation. As stated earlier, the goal of agreement requires an act of will and is a normative commitment. Argumentation itself is an exchange of information; agreement is one of many things that can be achieved with information. When the exploration of a position is seen not as a means to defeating an opposing claim, but as an opportunity to view the world the way one's dispute partner does, then agreement becomes a more likely outcome.

One word concerning inquiry; this endeavor, sometimes also referred to as 'dialectic,' is viewed as the most pure form of argumentation (Walton, 1989; van Eemeren & Grootendorst, 1988). It is in the realm of inquiry that bias is abandoned and the pursuit of truth is embraced. But we must doubt if this ever occurs in its pristine form, if we are ever capable of truly separating ourselves from all ego involvement, from all eristic elements, and from all task influences. This is not to say that inquiry never occurs, but rather, as suggested above, that it is a question of degree as opposed to something that happens as a matter of simple agreement between the participants. Inquiry is not empty ideal, but it is an ideal. As such, we have to allow that it does involve real speakers and hearers with real attachments and connections, biases and attitudes. Barring the few (if any) individuals truly capable of rising above it all, most instances of attempted inquiry are going to carry with them at least some of the baggage and difficulties of other sorts of argumentation.

It is more likely that argument involves, in the normal course of events, varying forms of argumentation in its distinct stages. Inquiry may well enter when we are trying to determine the nature of a dispute partner's position, persuasion dialogue when trying to convince them to soften a stand, and negotiation when trying to find a common ground of agreement.[43] In any given circumstance, one may be more important or central than another, but it is certainly possible that all have a role to play. In a "straight" negotiation, for example, inquiry may still play a vital role in the exploration of each party's position. A labor negotiation that commences with both parties inquiring into the state of the company is liable to have a greater chance of success than one that begins with opposing views that are not explored conjointly. Similarly, two social scientists inquiring into the effect of divorce on the educational careers of children may be well advised to investigate their attitudes and personal history in regard to these matters.

---

[43]This particular progression was suggested to me in a student essay submitted by Ms. Tara Smith (1993/1994) in my course, "Introduction to Argumentation Theory."

Finding agreement within argumentation is often difficult. The extent to which we focus on disagreement, and the degree to which we focus on initial claims as opposed to the exploration of the full matrix of a position will have a major impact on results. When argumentation is viewed as an exchange of information centered on disagreement, rather than a straightforward occasion to change someone's mind, opportunities for agreement will present themselves.

9

Applying Coalescent Argumentation

There are a multitude of different kinds of arguments that occur between people. Some ideal few are inquiries or critical discussions where the object is to determine the truth of a position or the value of a view. This might happen in an academic setting where, say, the question of the epistemological importance of feminism or the ability to create specific carbon compounds is at issue. Inquiries might also occur in business settings where a group is attempting to determine the risks in production expansion or the costs of employee retrenchment. Interpersonally as well, a couple experiencing marital difficulties can certainly attempt to consider their problems in the manner of an inquiry or critical discussion. Each of these arguments can, on analysis, be placed at some specific point on the heuristic/eristic scale. As attachment and various contextual factors come into play, the eristic component will increase or diminish.

Although some arguments begin with at least the avowed intention of following a heuristic path, others begin as highly eristic encounters. Sometimes one partner (Pro) to the dispute has what he thinks is a clear strategic goal and sets out to do whatever he can to achieve it without paying heed to his partner's (Con) goals or needs. If Pro runs into opposition and does not backtrack to a more heuristic approach, then the argument has the potential to devolve into a quarrel or row.

Still other arguments begin with the knowledge that there will be a conflict of goals, and that both Pro and Con will have to give something up in order to satisfy some parts of their goal set. These arguments, negotiations, can also have highly differing degrees of heuristic and eristic intent. Merely knowing in advance that one will have to move one's position in no way entails argumentative procedures that are coalescent. A negotiator can be intransigent, not bother to discover her opposer's position or goals, employ duplicitous methods, and otherwise proceed in bad faith.

Coalescent Argumentation offers to each of these types of argumentation a mode of proceeding that increases the heuristic component so that both parties have a greater expectation of maximizing their goals. Use of the procedures assumes that inquiry, along with the other forms of argument, can be opened up to include non-logical modes as legitimate components of the process. That is, rather than putting the non-logical elements aside, they are treated as part and parcel of the process. Accepting the platform of multi-modal argumentation means that emotional, visceral, and kisceral arguments and elements can be used to move toward a greater increase of heuristic content or toward a lessening of them.[44] There is always, of course, a choice that is inherent in the normative nature of coalescent argumentation. Just as one can choose to be polite or rude, so one can choose to be cooperative or antagonistic, and the reasons for the morally better behavior are also analogous. Just as one usually achieves more with politeness than rudeness, so one normally does better with cooperation than with antagonism as the latter is invariably met with a response in kind (see, for example, Axelrod, 1984).

It must be reiterated at this point that coalescent argumentation offers no promises concerning success. For one thing, even the most avowed coalescer can run into dispute partners who are totally antagonistic and eristically oriented. In addition, even when both partners are committed to a coalescent encounter, various factors, such as attachment and deeply seated dark-side commitments, can foil their best intentions. Even the most highly trained communicator will lose his perspective, temper, and grip on himself. But, even in these situations, there are liable to be pluses from reliance on coalescent argumentation. At the very least one should leave an encounter with a clearer understanding of an opposer's position and of the issues and goal conflicts separating the two sides. Moreover, one will have been reminded to examine the various levels of agreement and disagreement, and so have a deeper view of the dispute as it moves from mode to mode. Even in a relatively pure inquiry, attention to the various modes will provide insights into aspects of the position that might otherwise be overlooked. Consequently, using coalescent procedures will benefit an arguer even when the results are not all one might have wished.

Coalescent Procedures

The coalescent approach can be expressed in the very simplest of terms. First, expose the positions of the dispute partners; second, find the points of commonality; third, beginning from those points, attempt to explore means of maximizing the satisfaction of goals that are not in conflict and explore ways of satisfying goals that are apparently in conflict. Goals can be in conflict for many different reasons. However, the two most general categories are lack of resources, i.e., two people want the same non-divisible product; or, the goals are inherently in opposition, i.e., one excludes the other. In all cases, it is the careful exploration of goals, especially

---

[44]There is no assumption being made that using non-logical modes invariably leads to a 'better' argument. The alternative modes, just like the logical mode, can be used properly or improperly.

goals on different levels, that is liable to open up the possibilities of coalescence. Even in the most clinical and abstract of inquiries, learning how the contested proposition fits into a partner's broader scheme, and understanding what general significance that scheme has for the partner can lead to alternatives and avenues otherwise left unexplored.

The first rule of procedure for Coalescent Argumentation is to be aware of one's own positions. That is, prior to engaging in a dispute one should be familiar with what one wants. This gives us:

Prior to Encounter

1. Proponent (Pro) should know her/his position prior to stating agreement or disagreement.
   a. What is Pro's apparent strategic goal (ASG)?
   b. What are primary face goals?
   c. What are primary strategic goals?

Often arguments are not planned or scheduled, so one may not have much or any warning that a dispute is commencing. Nonetheless, the barest reflection, even on commencement, can render an argument much more highly focused. Moreover, it is vital that one consider both strategic and face goals. It is easy to pretend that there are no face goals in a given interaction, but, in fact, there always are. They need not be overwhelming, but then the task goal need not be held dearly either—some arguments are not as important as others. Naturally, the more one knows about one's position, especially about acceptable alternatives, the better off one is. However, we cannot demand too much, especially as one of the greatest benefits of argumentation is just that: one explores a position and examines its alternatives and connections to other positions.

Once the argument has commenced, it is crucial to learn as much as possible about the opposer's position. This will open up the possibilities of examining the goal sets to determine which goals, if any, lay within the intersection.

Discovering Con's Position

2. Determine the opposer's (Con) position before stating disagreement.
   a. What is Con's ASG?
   b. What face goals might be operative for Con?
   c. What task goals seem paramount to Con?

Notice that Con's position is, ideally, examined *prior* to the assertion of disagreement by Pro. On one level, this is the classic rule that one never agrees or disagrees with a claim, only with reasons for it. But it is intended to go further than that. First, it legitimates the role of face goals and acknowledges that Con will have them. Secondly, the focus on goals means that the objectives of the dispute are to be examined and not merely the mechanics. A position is a nexus of beliefs, values, attitudes and feelings. In uncovering a position one can begin to understand why Con holds the position, and, as a result of that, begin to explore alternative and mutually acceptable paths.

Identifying Commonality

  3. Identifying common elements.
  a. Do Pro and Con share strategic goals?
  b. Do Pro and Con share face goals?

The answers to questions 3a and 3b will, almost invariably, be, "yes."[45] The mere fact that two people are arguing is an indication of some shared concerns and values; we rarely, if ever, argue when there is true incommensurability. In the case of limited resource arguments, one shared goal will be the mutual desire to possess the resource. If we both want to use the car tomorrow, become senior vice president, go to the party with Astrid, or not be the one spending all weekend writing up the report, then, if nothing else, we value the same items, appreciate their worth, and, presumably, can understand how someone else would desire the same ends. In the case of exclusive goals, we must go back behind the exclusivity to examine the bases for the individual choices. If you want Peter to get the promotion while I favor Dorene, or I want a stop sign placed at the corner and you believe it's too expensive, or I think our holiday should be a wilderness canoe trip while you prefer a resort in Bermuda, then we must go back behind the choices to find the values on which they are based. It is there that the commonality will be found.

If one encounters difficulty in locating commonality of position between two partners, then it becomes important to examine the modes that are at work in the dispute. This serves two purposes. First, it can focus the disagreement by clarifying where it begins, and secondly, it can sometimes illustrate that the relevant goals are actually in different modes and not necessarily in competition. A dispute about a new stop sign might, for one partner, be a highly emotional issue concerning the safety of children, while for the other partner it is a logical matter concerning budgets and finances. The awareness that the partners are talking on different levels can allow them to find agreement on the issues, e.g., the value of children and the limitation of financial resources, and then, given these jointly respected parameters, begin to look for mutual solutions.

---

[45]I am avoiding declarations that might be unnecessarily strong. Thus, although I believe that all arguers will share some goals no matter how insignificant, I do not want to preclude the possibility there may be people who argue, but who are so far apart in their beliefs, values, and etc. that there is absolutely nothing in common. To do so would be to challenge the reader to find exceptions.

Examining Modes

4. Examining operative modes.
a. Are Pro and Con operating on the same mode?
b. Is the heart of the disagreement on the primary mode?
c. Might utilization of other modes be helpful?

Other aspects of modes are relevant as well. Sometimes dispute partners may both be operating on the same mode, but it is not the most useful mode. This commonly occurs when two arguers are remaining on the logical level when the emotional level is what is really at issue. This can often be identified by an undertone of emotionality kept hidden beneath a facade of logicality. In these, and other situations, the introduction of other modes can be very useful to the full expression of the positions and the location of commonality.

Exploring Depth

5. Examining depth of goals.
a. If primary goals are in conflict, explore secondary goals.
b. If goals are in conflict explore motives, values, and etc.

Procedure 5 comes into play primarily when the dispute has run into difficulties. The modes have been opened up to a horizontal investigation; that is, more than one mode is being explored, but there are still no indications that agreement is near. In that case, the remaining possibility is to explore one or more modes in a vertical manner by looking for deeper levels where agreement and/or understanding may be located. If exploring emotions is not helpful, then examining the attitudes and even deep feelings on which they rest may be fruitful. If we look to Table 8.2, it becomes clear that each mode has deeper levels of analysis that can be explored in order to locate a foundation for agreement from which the argument can proceed.

It is important at this point that various examples be examined in order to show how Coalescent Argumentation can work. Most of the examples are constructed, and all present difficulties: it is very easy to claim of any example that proceeds in a coalescent manner that it is contrived, and of any direction offered by the theory in a non-coalescent situation that it need not be followed. Both claims are true. Their truth lies in the simple fact that one is never under a logical obligation to follow any normative system whatsoever. But it must be remembered that Coalescent Argumentation is an avowedly normative undertaking, and, therefore, relies for its utilization on the goodwill of the participants, as well as their belief that proceeding in a coalescent fashion does, ultimately, achieve greater and more enduring results. For convenience, the five procedures introduced in the preceding sections will be presented again.

Coalescent Procedures

Prior to Encounter
1. Proponent [Pro] should know her/his position prior to stating agreement or disagreement.
a. What is Pro's apparent strategic goal [ASG]?
b. What are primary face goals?
c. What are primary strategic goals?

Discovering Con's Position
2. Determine the opposer's [Con] position before stating disagreement.
a. What is Con's ASG?
b. What face goals might be operative for Con?
c. What task goals seem paramount to Con?

Identifying Commonality
3. Identifying common elements.
a. Do Pro and Con share strategic goals?
b. Do Pro and Con share face goals?

Examining Modes
4. Examining operative modes.
a. Are Pro and Con operating on the same mode?
b. Is the heart of the disagreement on the primary mode?
c. Might utilization of other modes be helpful?

Exploring Depth
5. Examining Depth of goals.
a. If primary goals are in conflict, explore secondary goals.
b. If goals are in conflict explore motives, values, and etc.

Examples

The following examples attempt to illustrate the procedures in real life situations. In some instances, particular procedures will be emphasized, although it should be remembered that, in reality, things rarely happen one after another as in a model. This first example illustrates a situation in which one arguer needs to "back up" to explore goals in order to save the argument from deterioration.

The Van   (9.1)

Fran and David are discussing what sort of delivery vehicle their new pastry business should purchase. David has been pushing for a re-built antique panel truck decorated in turn of the century style. Fran has her eye on a used Ford van at one third that cost.

1. Fran: There's no good reason to spend a fortune on something like that; stop being silly.

2. David: I'm not being silly. It's beautiful, and I want it.

3. Fran: All right, all right. Just why do you want that van?

   Fran has stopped herself to go back and check for goals.

4. David: Because it says a lot about us. It says we're authentic, real, and just like our pastries use real ingredients, so does our delivery van.

   David's goal is to advertise something specific about the business and the way it operates.

5. Fran: A sign saying our ingredients are all natural would do the same and be a lot cheaper.

   Fran suggests an alternate way to achieve the same goal.

6. David: You don't get it. We can say 1,000 times that we're real and authentic, and we'll sound like everyone else. But *show it* once and they'll believe you forever.

   David is not so much denying that Fran has the correct goal, but rather that her way of securing it is faulty.

7. Fran: That's fine and well, and you might even be right, but the cost is just prohibitive.

   Now Fran has put her goal out more clearly: keep costs down.

8. David: That's a false economy, Fran—if we don't do it right we won't do it at all.

9. Fran: Fine, but I'm already terrified of how much I've got invested in this. If we put more in ...

   The argument is now moving to a discussion of emotions: Fran has backed up her logical statement with an emotional declaration. The discussion may now move to that level.

Procedure 1 stresses the importance of knowing one's own goals. This sounds easy, but is misleadingly difficult. One must not merely recognize one's ASG, but also identify alternate goals, conflicting goals, and subsidiary goals, whether they be task oriented or face oriented. Goals are almost always opposed to each other. David's desire to purchase a van that demonstrates the partners' commitment to quality and authenticity needs to be brought out. His goal may well be in conflict with Fran's desire to keep escalating costs in check. But, by bringing out their goals they may, at least, find ways to respect each other's needs. When Fran steps back and tries to determine David's goal, she is then in a situation to lay her own out as an opposed position. Once the goals can be seen in their conflicting way, progress can begin. As the discussion continues past turn [9], they should and will deal with their feelings regarding the way in which they present themselves and the frightening costs involved. There is no way to simply make this into a straightforward logical business decision. To do so would be to ignore the egos and feelings, and, thereby, lay the seeds of later difficulties.

It is also worth noting that not every conflict can be either anticipated or decided in advance. The intricacies of a conflict for Fran between the flashiness of the van and its cost require details that are impossible to anticipate. So, saying that one should know one's position in advance should not be taken simplistically. One thing one might know is that there may be some difficult choices in the offing. But the awareness that one's goals might well be in conflict diminishes the likelihood of surprise.

In the following example, Arnold has not considered his alternate goals and has a much reduced chance of finding a ground on which he and his wife can meet.

Holidays—The Beginning   (9.2)

"Why," Arnold demands, "do we always have to spend our holidays with your parents."

"Because," Sylvia replies, "they're old, they live far away, and it's the only chance I get to see them."

"But I want to do something else for once."

"Arnold, I have no choice. They're my parents." At this Arnold grimaces and storms off.

Leaving a dispute because one's ASG is not immediately satisfied is a mistake. Arnold hears Sylvia say that his primary goal will not be reached, so he abandons the interaction. If, however, he continues, he allows for the possibility of examining his and Sylvia's goals in a way that might allow for at least some mutual satisfaction. Questions about his goals remain open: Does he require the entire vacation period? Does all or part of the vacation have to be with Sylvia? Can Sylvia's parents travel with them? Can some other time be found when they can go off alone together or is this time particularly important? Since Arnold has not explored these possibilities himself, it is not likely he can work them out with Sylvia.

The second procedure is also essential to constructive communication, yet is one of the least honored of coalescent techniques. It is all too common for a protagonist to begin attacking an antagonist's position or attempting to change a dispute partner's mind *before fully identifying the partner's position.* Without understanding the position, without identifying the goals, beliefs and values involved in it, it is, to say the least, difficult to make coalescent progress. To use a slogan, it is impossible to change someone's mind if you do not know what it is.

What's In a Name   (9.3)

Liisa and Cynthia are approaching a discussion concerning the name change of a club newsletter. Cynthia wants the name altered to reflect a recent merger of their club with another, as well as other changes the club has undergone. She knows that Liisa is not happy with the idea of such a change.

1. Cynthia: Liisa, why do you think changing the name from *The Weaver's Club Newsletter* to *Woven Words Magazine* is a bad idea?

   Cynthia begins by trying to determine Liisa's position and goals.

2. Liisa: Because the old name has a certain tradition. There are connections to it, and I don't like throwing out the old for no good reason.

3. Cynthia: I can sympathize with that, but we are a new club, aren't we?

4. Liisa: Yes, but that doesn't mean we shouldn't keep some connection to the past.

   Liisa is sticking to her position and her motive.

5. Cynthia: But since the name of the club is totally different, shouldn't the magazine reflect that? I mean we aren't called *The Weaver's Club* anymore, so maybe the old name on the magazine should change?

6. Liisa [with some heat]: And why call it a magazine? What's wrong with "newsletter"? Why change everything?

Cynthia is nonplussed by this turn. Liisa seems to be overreacting, which may mean that there is something going on at a deeper level or in a different mode..

7. Cynthia: Why does calling it a magazine change anything? It just sounds classier, don't you think?

More information about Liisa's position is needed.

8. Liisa: It sounds harder, that's what. I edited a newsletter for two years, and now everyone wants me to edit a magazine! That's a lot bigger job.

Now Cynthia begins to see Liisa's problem. The name change represents more to Liisa than just a new title.

9. Cynthia: I see. So calling it a magazine makes it feel like a lot more responsibility?

10. Liisa: Magazines are big and glossy. I can't do something like that. What do I know about it?

Now, having gotten further down into what is at the root of Liisa's position, they might be able to find some way through the argument.

By not beginning with disagreement a coalescent arguer allows a partner to express what is important to him or her. Learning this is useful even when it may not reveal the entire or real goals of the partner. Note that Liisa's original goals dealt with maintaining traditions, and only on probing were other, underlying goals brought out. Initial goals and positions are important because if a dispute partner has other, nonexpressed goals and is consciously or unconsciously using the original reasons as a smokescreen, then difficulties found when probing the stated goals can bring forth the deeper, dark-side commitments not immediately expressed. In other words, the veridicality of the goals is not a necessary condition to their usefulness. Naturally, the more the stated goals have to do with the actual goals, the better. But not expecting actual goals is no reason not to pursue them.

Arnold, unlike Cynthia, has no interest in bringing out his wife's goals. His concentration is exclusively on his ASG. This, of course, makes compromise, negotiation, or the examination of alternative plans and avenues a waste of time. Arnold does not know what Sylvia wants, so he cannot try to fulfill her needs in a way other than the one she has identified.

Holidays—What I Want   (9.4)

After storming for a bit Arnold has returned to the discussion. "All right, I know they're your parents, but, I'm part of your family too. I want a holiday with you on the beach in Jamaica, and I've got as much right as they do."

Of course, Arnold might get his way pursuing this line of argument. Sylvia might give in, might even see Arnold's point of view without his presenting it in a coalescent way. On the other hand, Sylvia may well view Arnold's position as selfish and inconsiderate. *Arnold has no way of knowing.* He has not structured the dispute in a way that would reveal this information to him. Most importantly, he has not created a situation supportive of stage three of the procedures: finding commonality. By insisting on his goals rather than investigating Sylvia's, Arnold does not invite her to open up other modes where communication might be richer. Rather than, for example, allowing that she, too, would like a vacation away from her parents, she feels that admission would weaken her position as opposed to leading them to a coalescent encounter.

An Extended Example

The next example is examined in detail. In fact, it is examined several times with different twists. The example posits a hiring in a department of psychology. The protagonist is Laura, a tenured full professor who is eager to have a woman hired. She also has concerns about the hire's area, but they are not as relevant here. She is discussing this issue with Lane, an untenured recent male appointee who has personally been on the front lines of the affirmative action situation. We join the conversation after the usual non-phatic chit-chat.

Laura & Lane—A   (9.5)

Laura has run into Lane, their newest, youngest (and untenured) appointment. After the usual pleasantries, Laura broaches the topic of the upcoming hire.

A1. Laura: So, it's really good news that we got a new appointment, isn't it?

A2. Lane: It's great. I didn't think it would happen.

A3. Laura: Well, it gives us a chance to hire a woman so we can get our numbers up to somewhere decent.

Laura, in this version, has shown her goal right away, and, in particular, prior to identifying Lane's.

A4. Lane: [He frowns and hesitates before speaking.] Well, I didn't know that.

Lane's discomfort is palpable. It should be explored. How do Laura's goals and Lane's goals or feelings conflict?

A5. Laura: It's not the only reason we got the appointment, but it's certainly part of the agenda.

Laura has ignored Lane's signals and bulled on.

A6. Lane: Whose agenda? Mine is to get the best person available so we can have the best department possible.

At this point it seems as if their goals are opposed, though what Lane has indicated must be part of Laura's goal set as well.

Laura's approach violated several precepts of coalescent argumentation by not investigating Lane's position prior to asserting her own, especially since she has presented her position quite strongly. In doing so, she has made it more difficult to find joint goals that might allow for a position they could both live with. After A6, she could move to accept Lane's goal regarding the department, and begin to include some of her own. But a better approach would be one that begins with the establishment of Lane's goals like that demonstrated in the next sequence that begins anew at A3.

Laura & Lane—B   (9.6)

B3. Laura: What are your thoughts about it? Any wishes?

B4. Lane: Well, I guess the most important thing is to get the best person possible.

B5. Laura: I agree completely that getting a really good person is the most important thing. But, what about other considerations, like area?

There is now, at the beginning, a shared goal, even though Laura has modified it slightly.

B6. Lane: Well, that's complex. It depends to a certain extent on teaching needs, graduate demands, and stuff like that.

Lane is indicating that his goals in this area are not well defined.

B7. Laura: Right. And what about gender? Is that a consideration?

This time Laura has made a query rather than an assertion.

B8. Lane: [Looks troubled and hesitates.] Honestly? I'd like to see it go to the best candidate. If that's a male, then he should get it.

Note that this is a motive rather than a goal insofar as it guides decisions rather than makes them.

B9. Laura: But sometimes it's a close call ...

B10. Lane: And you think that then it should go to the woman.

Lane has identified Laura's goal which she has, in fact, presented implicitly.

B11. Laura: There were many, many years when the woman who was the best candidate didn't get the job.

B12. Lane: I know. And I know it was wrong. I just don't know that some guy who wasn't there should be the one to pay. I mean, I'm perfectly aware that my job was first offered to a woman who took a different position, and frankly, I think my dossier was better than hers.

This is said with some heat, a definite raise in emotional temperature.

B13. Laura: Maybe, maybe not. But you did get the job. And it's still true that there are many more men in the department than women. And the way you feel now is how thousands of women felt over the years.

Laura acknowledges Lane's distress, but is not empathizing. Instead, she is using an argument by analogy which, while in the same mode—women felt as you feel—might not serve her well.

Turn B13 is unfortunate because there was little Lane said in B12 that required Laura's disagreement. He began first by agreeing that previous discrimination was wrong, and then expressed concerns about who was to now pay the penalty. His next comment regarding his dossier in comparison to that of the person actually hired required no reply at all if for no other reason than such discussions are confidential. So Laura only needed to deal with the remark regarding the "some guy" who has to pay the price. Even here, however, there is room for agreement insofar as Laura certainly does not *want* any particular individual to suffer. Rather she wants a woman to be hired when there is a close call. She could very well regret the impact it has on a man and sympathize with Lane over the increased anxiety he felt when applying for jobs. This could, *later*, be connected to the same phenomenon, as it applied to women prior to affirmative action and the scrutiny of hiring. However, Laura is well-advised to postpone making the analogy until she has first demonstrated her ability to understand his feelings on the issue. She would be better advised to move to the emotional mode and determine what Lane's emotional goals or needs are.

In the following continuation, recommencing with turn C13 following Lane's B12, Laura will explore Lane's emotional situation before trying to change it.

Laura & Lane—C   (9.7)

C13. Laura: Well, I can't speak about dossiers, but I know it feels pretty awful when you know that it's not just your qualifications that are being considered. I don't envy the situation a male applicant is in.

Laura is identifying with Lane's feelings which permits him to expand on them.

C14. Lane: It feels as if you are being penalized for something you had nothing to do with.

C15. Laura: And that's true—you did have nothing to do with it.

Here Laura can now agree. Notice that she validates Lane's feelings and also reaffirms his blamelessness.

C16. Lane: I just wish we could get past all this already.

C17. Laura: Me too, and I hope when there's more balance in most departments, then we can just treat everyone the same.

In this sequence Laura has joined their positions by focusing on agreement. Now they both want the need for affirmative action to end, and both feel that there are hardships for people who have committed no wrongdoing. From here, they can go on to discuss the advantages of the appointment of a woman, and clarify just how the decision might be made if it is close. In addition, Laura might connect the discrimination women suffered previously, to the feelings Lane has about men being objects of discrimination. By holding off on disagreement and focusing on agreement, Laura has shown respect for Lane's feelings and found grounds on which they might move to a coalescent position.

Examples Concluded

The most ideal circumstance occurs when both parties are committed to working within a coalescent argumentation framework, but significant progress can also be made even when only one partner to the dispute uses coalescent techniques. In the following sequence Sylvia attempts to deal with Arnold's holiday disappointments.

Holidays—Talking–A   (9.8)

A1. Sylvia: Arnold, please, sit down and let's talk about this together?

A2. Arnold: Why? What's the point? Talking won't change anything. We'll still end up spending our holiday at your parents' cabin.

A3. Sylvia: Maybe, but maybe there's some way we can both be happy? I mean, I really feel obligated to see my parents, and you want to spend a holiday just the two of us.

This clearly states Sylvia's ASG and Arnold's as well.

A4. Arnold: Right, and we can't do both.

Arnold is viewing the positions a mutually exclusive, not without some warrant.

A5. Sylvia: Isn't there any way we can combine both?

A6. Arnold [with some heat]: Sylvia! We're in a cabin in the woods with them. There's no place to go! We spend virtually all our time with each other.

A7. Sylvia: I know. We're hardly ever alone on these holidays. It would be nice ... I mean, I hope you know that I'd like that too?

Sylvia is establishing commonality. Shared goals can lead to shared solutions.

A8. Arnold: Then why don't we just do it?

Arnold is still focused on the one solution—a vacation without Sylvia's parents.

A9. Sylvia: Because I've had a strong feeling for a while that Dad's not going to be around much longer. There's something in him that's slowing down ...

This is a kisceral argument.

A10. Arnold: He seems fine to me ...

A11. Sylvia: [thoughtfully] No. He's getting tired; I can sense it. That's one reason I don't want to stop seeing them now.

Like many kisceral arguments, this one is difficult to respond to. Sylvia is bound to know and be in deeper contact with her father than Arnold.

A12. Arnold: Okay, okay! I know if we didn't holiday with them and then he passed away you'd never forgive yourself—or me.

Arnold respects Sylvia's fears and, even if he does not accept the validity of her intuition, he accepts the consequences of being in error.

A13. Sylvia: But I *do* feel bad. It is your holiday too ...

A14. Arnold: If only we weren't all trapped together in that cabin ...

Now that cooperation is occurring the possibilities of freer expression may lead to unconsidered alternatives.

A15. Sylvia: Well, that's true ... [Sylvia and Arnold look at each other.]

A new idea is forming.

A16. Arnold: I mean, if we were at a hotel, say by a beach, then we wouldn't have to be together all the time.

A17. Sylvia: And then, after dinner, we
could go dancing and ...

A18. Arnold: and the walls wouldn't be
so thin ...

When people realize that they have shared goals, the energy that would go into defending and protecting a position can be released toward finding alternative solutions to shared problems.

In this last example, a typically trivial issue does not get out of hand because the participants are using coalescent techniques.

Getting Home   (9.9)

Holly and Lynn are working out their transportation arrangements for the evening. They have one car between them; present is a friend, Gloria.

1. Holly: So, what's happening tonight? Are you going to your class?

2. Lynn: Of course, I don't want to miss   *Both ASGs have been laid*
it. But you really need to go to that   *out—Holly's going to the meeting*
meeting.   *and Lynn's going to class.*

3. Holly: But then you can't get home.   *Now there's a conflict between*
ASGs.

4. Lynn: I'll get home.

5. Holly: Never mind, "I'll get home."   *Holly introduces another goal. No-*
That's a lousy neighborhood. I need   *tice that it does not conflict with any*
to know how you're getting home.   *other stated goal.*

6. Lynn: Don't worry so much.   *Lynn is not respecting Holly's anxi-*
ety; she would do better to move to
the emotional mode.

7. Holly: Listen—you're getting home   *Holly has now demonstrated that,*
safely is more important to me than   *given having to choose between*
going to that meeting. So, if we can't   *certain goals, she will pass on the*
work something out, you take the car   *meeting.*
and I'll stay home.

8. Lynn: But you should go to that meeting.

Lynn's goal is redeclared.

9. Holly: Then we have to figure something out.

Holly reasserts the conflict and her choice.

10. Gloria: Wait. Why don't *I* pick Lynn up after the meeting, and then, Holly, you can come and collect her at my place?

Gloria offers a way to satisfy both of Holly's goals.

11. Lynn: Wouldn't that be a lot of trouble for you? [Gloria shakes her head, no.] Then that works for me.

12. Holly: Yeah, but that's an awful lot of driving around for me.

The only solution found so far has an extra cost.

13. Lynn: [Looks at Holly pointedly.] It's not *that* much driving.

Lynn here points out that goal satisfaction is rarely perfect.

14. Holly: Good plan. I'll pick you up at Gloria's.

This example illustrates how a trivial discussion can keep from becoming a squabble by remaining focused on goals. Had the argument turned from the concrete goals at hand to other, less central issues, there is no telling where it might have ended. But, by remaining focused on the goals of the participants, Gloria was able to come to the rescue. Had the argument taken detours, she might have felt that it was inappropriate.

Coalescent Argumentation is not a way to happily resolve every argument one ever has. It is a way to keep arguments on track and help prevent them from devolving into less ideal forms such as quarrels or squabbles.

10

Concluding Remarks

Coalescent Argumentation has a number of key assumptions that drive the theory. One is that every arguer has a complex set of goals. Another, less absolute, is that these goals will range over more than one modality. The third, is that the most general goal of the activity of argumentation is agreement. To begin this chapter I would like to consider this last assumption.

Agreement as Ideal End

There are a number of situations one can imagine in which agreement is not the apparent primary or even secondary goal. In contexts where Pro has no concern for Con's goals or desires, then the object is simply to persuade Con to accept a statement or its correlate action whether or not he or she agrees with the position. This might be done through intimidation, insinuation, emotional blackmail, relentless argumentation, or other means that in no way deal with an opposer's concerns. Of course, it can be said that even in these cases the goal is agreement, namely, getting Con to "agree" with the proffered claim and carry through with the connected activity. This kind of agreement, although it is unconnected to a sharing or thoughtful and negotiated movement, is agreement nonetheless. What it lacks is a consideration of the needs and goals of one's dispute partner. In other words, the outlook is not coalescence, but consists merely in the desire on the part of Pro to have Con agree with whatever Pro wants.

Arguments of the sort just described are classed as highly eristic, and they do have agreement as their goal, but not in the coalescent sense of the term. The arguer pressing the point is being shortsighted insofar as he or she is failing to recognize two things. First, the relationship between the arguers is at least as important as the ASG, and, secondly, by including Con's goals in the final agreement, Pro is more likely to get what he or she wants. But sometimes Pro is arguing with a stranger and has no interest in the continuing relationship, or the ASG is so monumental to Pro that there is no concern for other matters; that is, Pro cares so much about the

ASG that concerns about relationship goals become minor. This happens. Still, even in such highly eristic situations, agreement can be said to be the goal.

Is it then analytic that agreement is the goal of argument? Perhaps not. There are a number of argument categories where one might maintain that agreement is not the goal of the interaction. First, there is the devil's advocate argument, secondly, there is the "I want to be wrong" argument, and thirdly, there is Popperian scientific exploration. Let us consider these in turn.

The devil's advocate argument occurs when Con is attacking a position that he holds along with Pro in order to test the position against objections. This is done in many situations ranging from family decisions to major business moves. The idea is that Con will do his best to defeat the position while Pro does her best to defend it. If Con—as they both hope—fails in his attempt, then they can hold the position defended by Pro with increased confidence. But as soon as we consider the desired outcome it becomes clear that they want to agree, namely, that Con is wrong and Pro is right. Nor will they, largely, use coalescent procedures. The arguments used will be the most direct and challenging they can come up with in order to see if the position can withstand direct attack. Note, however, that I say "largely," because they might also want to use coalescent procedures in order to examine the effects on the position of an agreement based approach.

The second category is exemplified by arguments where Pro wants to be wrong. Imagine that I am convinced that the only way out of my financial difficulties is to declare personal bankruptcy, or, I own a small business and am convinced that I must lay off several employees or go under. In each case, I decide to discuss the matter with a professional counselor or a friend, and, in presenting my case, I want to be wrong. That is, I am hoping that I can be convinced that I missed some crucial point or that there is some alternative I had not seen. This is an inverse of the devil's advocate argument, insofar as the positions of attack and defense are the same, but the desired outcome is the opposite. Now, I want to end up agreeing with Con, rather than having Con decide I cannot be defeated. But, clearly, this form too ends up in agreement—with Con if the result is as wished, with Pro if otherwise.

Popperian Disagreement

The last category concerns the Popperian approach to scientific progress. Put simply, the view postulates that scientific hypotheses are put forward, then placed in a position where they can be falsified (Popper, 1979). If they are falsified, then they are abandoned and a newer, better view is adopted. This accounts for progress. On this view, the Popperian scientist wants to be wrong in order that progress be made. She does not, however, want to agree with her adversary because the position is, after all, hers. So there is a tension between the overarching desire for scientific progress and the individual need to have put forward a correct position. What makes sense in this case is a distinction between the individual instance and the longer term effect. The individual wants to have said something true, but believes that, in the long run, the view held will be superceded.[46] So, in the long run, it is disagreement that is best, but, in the short run, Pro seeks agreement as much as anyone else. It should also be noted that the best case scenario would have Pro reluctantly agreeing that the position must be given up or amended. So, here, too, agreement is the ideal final outcome.

It is important to stress that the Popperian falsification view (PFV) does emphasize the value of disagreement over that of agreement. Even if, in some more or less analytical sense, the ideal *end result* of argument is agreement, the best way to get there, on the PFV, is actually through fairly hard-nosed, analytical, even no-holds barred *disagreement*. The reasons for this view are several. First, the alteration of views held by individuals will be firmer and more stable if the change only occurs after involved and lengthy argumentation. Secondly, one should only give up a view when it is false, but falseness is, of course, a non-empirical property of positions. Falseness, like truth, is not manifest. So the only way to have confidence that an abandoned view actually is false is by having tried one's very best to argue for it's truth as strenuously and thoroughly as possible, and, of course, to have failed. If science and human knowledge are to progress, it is the very contest of positions, views, and beliefs that will be that very progress. By no means does this include looking for bases of agreement in order to find some common ground leading to an agreement that will make both parties happy. Knowledge, and, especially, science has nothing to do with happiness.

The PFV also needs to be distinguished from what I have called above the Natural Light Theory (NLT.) The NLT view holds that when two positions are in conflict, the one that is true will be the one that survives. The Popperian view, on the other hand, holds that the one that loses is the one that is false. It makes no claim about the surviving view being true. As a result, most contemporary observers, having witnessed how harsh the history of science is to views designated as 'true' tend more to a PFV than any other in their everyday approach to how things should be taken.

A proponent of the PFV would argue that Coalescent Argumentation is a wrongheaded approach liable to lead one into error and the hasty abandonment of positions. I allow that this may be true. That is, in some circumstances, notably highly linear quantitative circumstances, seeking an agreement in order to maximize the satisfaction of the parties to the dispute might not be the best way to proceed. Or, rather, it may not be advisable to utilize Coalescent Argumentation as the *exclusive* investigative tool.

---

[46]I have heard individual Popperians repeatedly state that they "want to be wrong," but, at the same time, they will defend their position vigorously and, in my experience, rarely, if ever, actually concede to being wrong. Of course, they are supposed to defend their positions because it is that tension that creates progress—a sort of institutional devil's advocate. It does, however, give one cause to pause and wonder if the Popperian saying, "Please, please, show me where I am wrong," doth protest too much.

Having said this, I hasten to add that it rarely happens. Realms of dispute have their own rules and procedures, and those circumstances in which coalescent argumentation is inappropriate tend to rule it out. Moreover, there are numerous situations in which coalescent argumentation is not used or is considered to be inappropriate where it ought have a role. In law, for example, coalescent argumentation is frequently considered to be antithetical to the adversarial system of courts found in North America and numerous other jurisdictions. However, in many situations, commercial as well as familial, mediation is being recommended as an alternative to litigation. Moreover, in the vast majority of interpersonal arguments people are involved in on a daily and regular basis, Coalescent Argumentation is by far the more appropriate approach. A further danger is that many individuals who utilize an adversarial technique professionally neglect to change over in more intimate surroundings, a fact which can cause a good deal of stress.[47]

In reality, most arguments considered to be scientific or highly technical are also subject to various kinds of negotiations, from the terms used and their meanings to assumptions granted for the sake of argument. In addition, many aspects of Coalescent Argumentation, such as the importance of understanding an opposer's position, paying attention to goals, and being aware of the modes on which argumentation is taking place are all valuable considerations for any kind of argument, whether the desired end goal is agreement or defeat of an opponent's position. One can also question, as I just have, whether the ideology that false theses are those that are defeasible is a valuable axiom. Perhaps there are theses that would stand humankind in good stead *even though* they cannot stand up to the severest of logico-rationalist onslaughts. One cannot be sure. However, it is possible that, as the *best* person is not always the strongest person, perhaps the best position is not always that which can most easily ward off attack.

Agree-Phobia

The fear, of course, is that by making agreement the end and be all of argumentation, and, hence of a good deal of communication, one is opening the door, so to speak, to a *folie de monde*, a sort of mass *folie á deux*, wherein the eagerness to agree overtakes the desire to be correct. On this model, agreements pile up one on another, regardless of the truth, the facts, or the reality of the situation simply because those involved are committed to agreeing. In a kind of feeding frenzy of agreement partners to a dispute simply ignore everything but their desire to agree. The result is, potentially, disastrous.

The view just expressed may or may not be a real concern to a theory that postulates agreement as the sole ground for argumentative communication. Coa-

---

[47]My own experience in teaching adult education courses shows that lawyers frequently bring the adversarial method of argumentation home. This can lead, if not corrected, to a great deal of stress, alienation and marital and familial discord.

lescent Argumentation, however, makes no such postulation. It is not that agreement, *in and of itself*, is such a wonderful objective, but that agreement arrived at as a result of the mutual respect of diverse and shared goals is a satisfying and enduring solution to a multitude of disagreements.

There certainly are innumerable *folie de monde* in a multitude of situations including some that are scientific, but this in no way can be laid at the door of Coalescent Argumentation. Groups and disciplines, as formed in fields, invariably have numerous presuppositions and knowledge claims that are taken as true and considered to be largely unchallengeable. This is a basic tenet of field theory and applies to physics as much as to religious cults. (See, Willard, 1983.) Nothing happens within communication without some degree of agreement, even if only with respect to the significance of issues, the salience of classes of evidence, and the concurrence as to the nature of basic facts. These beliefs, many of which, while held dearly by one group, are considered nothing less than absurd by another, are not created by the desire to find agreement, but rather the group itself is founded as a result of locating an initial agreement within itself. Certainly, coalescent procedures may occur within the group, but this is true of any field at all. Coalescent communication, like all communication, requires a foundation of initially shared beliefs and procedures.

Still, although the nagging question, "Well, why not just agree?" persists, there is a simple answer. That is, mere agreement does not often satisfy one's goals. Too often, the conflict is just over goals, and the mutual satisfaction of them requires attention to procedure. But people do sometimes agree when they do not really mean it, do they not? Yes, they do, but not often when anything major is at stake. I might agree to do you a favor when I am not really inclined to because I would rather not argue the point. I might agree to my mate's seating arrangement for a dinner party because I know this is more important to her than it is to me. I might agree to a plethora of things rather than argue them when the cost to me is minimal, i.e., the goals I have are not that significant, especially, perhaps, when compared to my partner's. But, surely, no one holds the position that everything should be argued to the full no matter how inconsequential? Were that the case, nothing would ever be accomplished.

Coalescent Argumentation in no way leads one to facile agreements for their own sake. On the contrary, while it is based in agreement as both a procedure and goal, the extent to which it takes seriously the goals and positions of both partners *enables* an agreement that maximizes satisfaction, but in no way encourages agreement that does not encompass the goals and respect the positions of both parties.

One final attempt before I move on to another issue. "Wait a minute," my interlocutor might say, "agreement is fine when there's partial right on both sides, but sometimes one 'partner' as you so rhetorically call them is just plain wrong. Why should I seek out agreement with someone who's just got it wrong?"

To begin with, let me agree that sometimes someone is just wrong. It does not happen that often, but happen it does, and when it does there is no reason to agree—unless, of course, that initial agreement can be what leads to showing the obvious fault of the position, the inconsistency, factual absurdity, or so on. If there is not such an obvious way to illustrate the wrongheadedness, then how can we be so certain that the position is so clearly at fault? In other words, if it really is definitely and obviously wrong, then there ought be no obstacles to the demonstration of same. If the demonstration is not simple, then the obviousness of the error must be brought into question. And, if the error is that obvious, and the demonstration that straightforward, but the proponent still refuses to accept, then one needs question either Con's claim that the position is so obviously wrong or Pro's ability to follow an argument. In either case, obviousness is a self-proclaiming property: If *P* is obvious to Con but not to Pro, then *P* is not, *ipso facto*, obvious, and the argument must be treated more seriously. Put another way, if my dispute partner thinks I'm obviously wrong, and I don't, then she has more work to do than she would like—but there's no help for it.

What Is Needed

One of the main, indeed, primary thrusts of Argumentation Theory and Informal Logic has been the careful analysis of arguments. For Argumentation Theory, the emphasis has been on dialogic argumentation, that is, argu*ing* as it occurs between people with differing positions and/or goals. Informal Logic has primarily, but not exclusively, examined particular arguments, i.e., claim-reason complexes (CRCs), with an eye to judging the strength and weaknesses of each particular argument. As discussed at length in chapter 3, there are difficulties with these approaches, especially the latter, that Coalescent Argumentation is intended to correct. But it must be understood that these approaches are valuable analytical tools, and it is not my intention that they be discarded or abandoned.

What has been lacking in the analysis of arguments as conducted by real people in real situations has not been lack of critical or logical rigor. Those arenas have received voluminous attention for myriad years. The most recent developments in Argumentation Theory have heralded a sophistication that is the result of a long concerted effort to treat argumentation as a multi-faceted and multi-disciplinary endeavor. Most particularly, the Pragma-Dialectic approach of the Amsterdam School, especially as evidenced in recent publications (van Eemeren, et al., 1993, 1996) approaches argumentation as something live and changing. Although these advances still fall prey to various difficulties raised by Willard and Gilbert, (Gilbert, 1995; Willard, 1989,) they do begin to take into account the contextual and human factors that have often been put aside.

Argumentation, to repeat a quote from Willard (1989), is a multifaceted human endeavor wherein, "arguers, like all communicators, employ the full range of available communication modalities, verbal and nonverbal, explicit and implicit" (p. 8). That means, if taken seriously, that we must analyze and consider as serious components of argument those non-linear, non-logical activities of communicative practice. So, it is not that the logical mode ought be dropped, but rather that the non-logical modes ought be examined and analyzed more closely. What is required, in fact, is the sort of careful, even rule based, method of analysis used in pragma-dialectics or detailed RSA analyses. If these sorts of approaches can be turned to the understanding of the emotional, visceral, and kisceral aspects of argumentation, then further advances in understanding can be expected. Hopefully, such work may be inspired by my own meager attempts to broaden current conceptions of the limits of Argumentation Theory.

More than anything else, Argumentation Theory, if it is to come to truly serve the needs of real situated arguers, must open the concept of rationality to include the non-logical modes as legitimate and respectable means of argumentation. This is important because these modes are actually used in marketplace argumentation. The simple observation of real arguments had by real people demonstrates that the range of arguments used goes well beyond the limited and quasi-logical argument forms certified as acceptable by narrower approaches. It is, of course, an advance when researchers say that the analytical tools are only intended to isolate one aspect or diagnostic approach to Argumentation Theory, but I question whether or not these claims are intended to truly allow for further expression. If non-logical communi-cations are generally lumped into some huge category of "other stuff" and not considered in detailed analyses, then it is hard to believe that their importance is being taken seriously.

Pragmatic Philosophy

There has been, for some time now, a movement in philosophy toward the more pragmatic. This has led to the emphasis of sub-disciplines that involve real actors involved in real activities. Evidence of this trend can be found in the enormous rise of practical ethics as an area of study. What began as a primarily pedagogic endeavor often tolerated only with indulgence, has become a major area of serious investi-gation. I also take the rise of feminist epistemology and related areas as an indication of the importance of the practical. Feminist approaches invariably rely more on the situated actor operating in an actual context formed of a web of concerns that interconnect relationships, the natural world, and individual historicity. This moves us away from the ideal and unrealizable notion that persons exist in the abstract without beliefs, goals, needs and desires. Whether persons commence their exist-ence as *tabula rasa,* or with explicit or implicitly programmed belief structures (dispositional or otherwise,) is certainly interesting and can be relevant to numerous issues and questions. But no one will ever enter into a dispute communication with a *tabula rasa,* so from the point of view of Argumentation Theory as opposed, say to psychological epistemology, the question is irrelevant.

The people we do argue with have full sets of beliefs, desires, needs and goals, and these are rarely, if ever, separable into neat epistemological categories. In real life, goals impinge on beliefs, desires color knowledge, and needs form a large part of the way in which we see the world. Coalescent Argumentation contains two major components, each of which takes this picture of people arguing *qua* people seriously.

Multi-modal argumentation which is, as it were, the metaphysics of Coalescent Argumentation, accepts as a reality that people do not argue from an exclusively logical or linear point of view. Rather, people's arguments may stem from their emotions, physicality, or intutions. These modes are labelled, respectively, the emotional, visceral, and kisceral. There may as I said earlier, be other ways to model the forms used, fewer or more categories might serve our purposes better. But these four modes seem to cover a wide range of human communicative activity in what is, I hope, a useful way. Arguments can be formed within a mode by using evidence in that mode, staking claim to information in that mode, using warrants specific to a given mode, or simply by being about something in a particular mode. Nor is there any necessary connection between subject matters and means of argumentation. There are arguments about religion, an inherently kisceral subject, that are highly logical, and arguments in astrophysics that are highly kisceral. There are no rules, and even if there were, no one would follow them. But perhaps this conclusion is hasty.

There are, in Argumentation Theory and Informal Logic, any number of systems of rules that are laid down for the edification and enlightment of those who would argue well and correctly. Arguing "well" in this context, invariably means arguing logically, generally dispassionately, and not infrequently with a fairly high degree of analytical content. In other words, arguing well seems to fall within the purview of logical argument. Nor is there anything wrong with a properly conducted logical argument. There is only something wrong when that is considered to be the only way there is to argue at all. It is not that we do not need rules, it is that we do not have enough of them. We need rules for non-logical argumentation: Rules of evidence, interaction, fallaciousness, and connectivity.

Rules are created by those of us who see argumentation as the most crucial path to the elimination of violence and the promotion of humanitarian values. But if these rules are to work, then they ought be created in such a way as to fit the reality of the human situation. If they are to intended to facilitate the betterment of the human lives, then they ought be connected to it in non-trivial ways.

If the only response to non-logical argumentation, to argumentation as it occurs in the other modes, is that it is fallacious, or ought be eliminated, or is really beside the point, then it will never be properly studied. Argument from the alternate modes will never have rules and procedures designed to foster good, constructive, coalescent argumentation until they are allowed as argumentation at all. So much seems obvious. But it also seems obvious that the argumentation theorist needs to examine argument as it actually happens, and not only as she or he thinks it ought to happen. Once that extra step is made, and the descriptive leap into the morass of reality is taken, then the full normative enterprise can begin.

In Praise of Normativity

The idea of coalescence is an explicitly normative one: Argue so as to maximize the goal satisfaction of both participants to the dispute. Note that the carrot and the stick are simple inverses: in most contexts one will do better than otherwise, and because in most contexts, one is arguing with an ongoing partner, the long-term consequences must also be taken into account. So, one ought to argue in a coalescent manner because one will do better in the long run, and if one does not, then one will do worse in the long run. Even in situations where one can dictate the result we know, as did Machiavelli (1952), that one is better off recognizing at least some of the goals of one's dispute partner. Cooperation may not always beget cooperation, but antagonism always begets antagonism.

The idea that philosophy is becoming more practical does not mean that it is no longer concerned with metaphysics, epistemology, or with the Great Questions. First, there should be and always will be room in the philosophical enterprise for the purely abstract and inapplicable. If not there, then where? But, and this is more to the point, more philosophers are doing philosophy in ways that touch upon the concerns of the person in the street. Feminist epistemology, Rortyian pragmatic metaphysics, and other approaches are all ways of building bridges between the ivory tower and the Clapham Omnibus, between Academe and the person on the street. Argumentation Theory, too, is such a bridge.

Normativity, if it is to succeed, needs to hold out a promise. It need not be something very concrete or quantifiable, but the idea that one will, at the least, get back as good as one gives, is typically embedded in normative directives. And so it is with coalescence: One is more likely to achieve some or all of one's goals if one attempts to satisfy some or all of one's partner's. But, there is a further reward that is not necessarily returned in kind. And that is an increase in the amount of cooperation that exists in the world as opposed to the amount of antagonism and distress. This is not a quantifiable return. But if we can move from the solution of problems by violence and toward their resolution and negotiation, then we have certainly made an important movement.

Argument is the best alternative to violence. And the more we treat argument as a full, rich, multi-faceted endeavor, the more we can appeal to real acting people to utilize it. When argumentation is considered rarefied and technical, the domain of academics, then it will not appeal greatly as an alternative. Only when it deals with the kinds of arguments, the kinds of warrants, moves, data, and realities that situated arguers are concerned with will it speak to people as a useful and authentic tool of non-conflictual communication.

Coalescent Argumentation is my meager attempt to find a path to a larger sense of argumentation that corresponds to the realities of marketplace arguers. I do not pretend to have moved very far in that direction with these poor considerations. But, if I have induced some theorists to consider the place of nontraditional modes of reasoning in the greater scheme of things, then I have helped the field progress. And if some few others proceed to consider the ideas of cooperation and agreement as being integral to constructive, heuristic argumentation, then, too, the field will have moved forward.

Coalescence is the bringing together of disparate views by focusing on their commonalities, the mutual goals held by the partners to the dispute, and a careful examination on all communicative levels to determine whether or not there truly is conflict. I believe that most of what I have written here is not in conflict with the prevailing theories in Argumentation Theory. Rather, there is room for coalescence, room for inclusion, and ample room for agreement. When we focus on what we share, we move forward and leave violent conflict behind us, and that, the elimination of violence as a response to disagreement is, and must be, the final aim of all Argumentation Theory

References

(Note: Prior to 1988, volume 25, the journal *Argumentation & Advocacy* was known as the *Journal of the American Forensic Association*.)

Axelrod, R. (1984). *The evolution of cooperation.* New York: Basic Books.

Barth, E. M., & Krabbe, E. C. W. (1982). *From axiom to dialogue.* Berlin: de Gruyter.

Balthrop, B. (1980). Argument as linguistic opportunity: A search for form and function. In J. Rhodes & S. Newell (Eds.), *Proceedings of the [1979] Summer Conference on Argumentation* (pp. 184–212). Annandale, VA: Speech Communication Association.

Bavelas, J. B. (1991). Some problems with linking goals to discourse. In K. Tracy (Ed.), *Understanding face to face interaction: Issues linking goals and discourse* (pp. 119–130). Hillsdale, NJ: Lawrence Erlbaum Associates.

Bavelas, J. B., & Black, A., & Chovil, N., & Mullet, J. (1990) Truth, lies, and equivocations. The effects of conflicting goals on discourse. In N. Coupland & K. Tracy (Eds.), *Multiple goals in discourse* (pp. 135–161). Avon, England: Multilingual Matters Ltd.

Bochenski, I. M. (1970). *A history of formal logic.* (2nd ed.). New York: Chelsea.

Brockriede, W. (1975). Where is Argument? *Journal of The American Forensic Association, XIII,* 129–132.

Brown, P., & Levinson, S. (1987). *Politeness: Some universals in language usage.* Cambridge, UK: Cambridge University Press.

Burleson, B. (1981). "The senses of argument revisited." In J. Rhodes & G. Ziegmuller (Eds.), *Dimension of Argument: Proceedings of the Second Conference on Argumentation* (pp. 955–979). Annandale, VA: Speech Communication Association.

Code, L. (1991). *What can she know?* Ithaca, NY: Cornell University Press.

Cody, M. J., & McLaughlin, M. L. (Eds.). (1990). *The psychology of tactical communication.* Avon, UK: Multilingual Matters Ltd.

Copi, I. M. (1961). *Introduction to logic.* (2nd ed.). New York: Macmillan.

Cox, J. R., & Willard, C. A., (1982). *Advances in argumentation theory and research.* Carbondale, IL: Southern Illinois University Press.

Craig, R., (1986). "Goals in discourse." In D. G. Ellis & W. A. Donohue (Eds.), *Contemporary issues in language and discourse processes* (pp. 257–273). Hillsdale, NJ: Lawrence Erlbaum Associates.

Dillard, J. P. (1990). The nature and substance of goals in tactical communications. In M. J. Cody & M. L. McLaughlin (Eds.), *The psychology of tactical communication* (pp. 69–90). Avon, UK: Multilingual Matters Ltd.

Eemeren, Frans van, & Grootendorst, R. (1982). Unexpressed premises: Part I. *Argumentation & Advocacy, 19*(2), 97–106.

Eemeren, Frans van, & Grootendorst, R. (1983). Unexpressed premises: Part II. *Argumentation & Advocacy, 19*(4), 215–225.

Eemeren, Frans van, & Grootendorst, R. (1984). *Speech acts in argumentative discussions*. Dordrecht, Holland: Foris Publishers.

Eemeren, Frans van, & Grootendorst, R. (1987). Fallacies in pragma-dialectic perspective. *Argumentation, 1*(3), 283–302.

Eemeren, Frans van, & Grootendorst, R. (1988). Rationale for a pragma-dialectical perspective. *Argumentation, 2,* 271–292.

Eemeren, Frans van, & Grootendorst, R. (1989). Speech act conditions as tools for reconstructing argumentative discourse. *Argumentation, 3*(4), 367–384.

Eemeren, Frans van, Grootendorst, R., & Kruiger, T. (1987). *Handbook of argumentation theory*. Dordrecht, Holland: Foris Publishers.

Eemeren, Frans van, & Grootendorst, R., & Jackson, S., & Jacobs, S. (1993). *Reconstructing argumentative discourse*. Tuscaloosa, AL: University of Alabama Press.

Eemeren, Frans van, Grootendorst, R., & Snoeck Henkemans, F. (1996). *Fundamentals of argumentation theory: Handbook of historical backgrounds and contemporary developments*. Mahwah, NJ: Lawrence Erlbaum Associates.

Ellis, D. G., & Donohue, W. A. (Eds.), 1986. *Contemporary issues in language and discourse processes*. Hillsdale, NJ: Lawrence Erlbaum Associates.

Engel, M. (1985). *With good reason: An introduction to informal fallacies* (3rd ed.) New York: St. Martin's Press.

Fogelin, R. J., & Sinnott-Armstrong, W. (1991). *Understanding arguments*. Orlando, FL: Harcourt Brace.

Friedman, M. (1987). Beyond caring: The demoralization of gender. *Canadian Journal of Philosophy, Supplementary Volume 13*. Calgary, Alberta: The University of Calgary Press.

Gilbert, M. A. (1979). *How to win an argument*. New York: McGraw-Hill.

Gilbert, M. A. (1991). The enthymeme buster: A heuristic procedure for position exploration in dialogic dispute. *Informal Logic, 13*(3), 159–166.

Gilbert, M. A. (1994). Multi-modal argumentation. *Philosophy of the Social Sciences, 24*(2), 159–177.

Gilbert, M. A. (1995). Arguments and arguers. *Teaching Philosophy, 18*(2), 125–138.

Gilbert, M. A. (1995a). Coalescent argumentation. *Argumentation, 9*(5), 837–852.

Gilbert, M. A. (1995b). Feminism, argumentation and coalescence. *Informal Logic, 16*(2), 95–113.

Gilbert, M. A. (1995c). The delimitation of "Argument." *Inquiry, 15*(1), 63–75.

Gilbert, M. A. (1996). *How to win an argument* (2nd ed.) New York: Wiley.

Gilligan, C. (1982). *In a different voice*. Cambridge, MA: Harvard University Press.

Gilovich, T. (1991). *How we know what isn't so*. New York: The Free Press.

Goffman, E. (1959). *The presentation of self in everyday life*. Garden City, NY: Doubleday.

Govier, T. (1987). *Problems in argument analysis and evaluation*. Dordrecht: Foris Publishers.

Govier, T. (1988). *A practical study of argument* (2nd ed.). Belmont, CA: Wadsworth.

Grice, P. (1989). Logic and conversation. In *Studies in the way of words*. (pp. ??–??). Cambridge, MA: Harvard University Press. (Original work published 1975)

Groarke, L., & Tindale, C. (1986). Critical thinking: How to teach *good* reasoning. *Teaching Philosophy 9*(4), 301–318.

Guthrie, W. K. C. (1971). *The sophists*. Cambridge University Press.

Hamblin, C. L. (1970). *Fallacies*. London: Methuen.

Hample, D., & Dallinger, J. (1992). The use of multiple goals in cognitive editing of arguments. *Argumentation & Advocacy, 28,* 109–122.

Hawkesworth, M. E. (1987). Feminist epistemology: A survey of the field. *Women & Politics, 7*(3), 115–127.

Jackson, S., & Jacobs, S. (1980). Structure of conversational argument: Pragmatic bases for the enthymeme. *The Quarterly Journal of Speech, LXVI,* 251–265.

Jacobs, S., & Jackson, S. (1982). Conversational argument: A discourse analytic approach. In J. R. Cox & C. A. Willard (Eds.), *Advances in argumentation theory and research* (pp. 205–237). Carbondale, IL: Southern Illinois University Press.

Jacobs, S. (1989). Speech acts and arguments. *Argumentation, 3*(4), 345–366.

Jacobs, S., Jackson, S., Stearns, S., & Hall, B. (1991). "Digressions in argumentative discourse: Multiple goals, standing concerns, and implicatures." In K. Tracy, (Ed.), *Understanding face to face interaction: Issues linking goals and discourse* (pp. 43–61). Hillsdale, NJ: Lawrence Erlbaum Associates.

Johnson, R. H. (1995). *The principle of vulnerability.* A paper presented at the Ontario Society for the Study of Argumentation, Ontario, Canada.

Johnson, R. H., & Blair, J. A. (1983). *Logical self-defense* (2nd ed.). Toronto: McGraw-Hill Ryerson.

Johnson, R. H., & Blair, J. A. (1987). Argumentation as dialectical. *Argumentation, 1*(1), 41–56.

Johnson, R. H., & Blair, J. A. (1993). *Logical self-defense* (3rd ed.) Toronto: McGraw-Hill Ryerson.

Kahane, H. (1971). *Logic and contemporary rhetoric: The use of reason in everyday life.* Belmont, CA: Wadsworth.

Kneale, W., & Kneale, M. (1962). *The development of logic.* Oxford: Clarendon Press.

Kneupper, C. W. (1981). Argument: A social constructivist perspective. *Journal of the American Forensic Association, 17,* 183–189.

Lakoff, R. T. (1990). *Talking power: The politics of language.* New York: Basic Books.

Legge, N. J. (1990). What did you mean by that?: The function of perceptions in interpersonal argument. *Argumentation and Advocacy, XXIX*(2), 41–60.

Machiavelli, N. (1952). *The prince* (L. Ricci, Trans., E.R.P. Vincent, revised trans). New York: New American Library.

Mannix, D. (1991). *Life skills activities for special children.* West Nyack, NY: Center for Applied Research in Education.

Moulton, J. (1983). A paradigm of philosophy: The adversary method. In S. Harding & M. B. Hintikka, *Discovering reality: Feminist perspectives on epistemology, and philosophy of science.* (Vol. 161, pp. 5–20). Dordrecht, Holland: D. Reidel.

Naess, A. (1953). *Interpretation and preciseness.* Oslo: Skrifter utgitt ar der norske videnskaps academie.

Naess, A. (1956). *Wie fordert man heute die empirische Bewegung?* Oslo: Universitetsforlaget.

Naess, A. (1966). *Communication and argument: Elements of applied semantics.* Oslo: Unversitetsforlaget.

Natanson, M., & Johnstone, H. W., Jr. (1965). *Philosophy, rhetoric and argumentation.* University Park, PA: The Pennsylvania State University Press.

Nye, A. (1990). *Words of power.* New York: Routledge.

O'Keefe, B., & McCornack, S. A. (1987). Message design logic and message goal structure. *Human Communication Research, 14,* 68–92.

O'Keefe, B. J. (1988). The logic of message design: Differences in reasoning about communication. *Communication Monographs, 55,* 80–103.

O'Keefe, B. J. (1996). Influence and identity in social interaction. *Argumentation, 9*(5), 785–800.

O'Keefe, B. J., & McCornack, S. A. (1987). Message design logic & message goal structure: Effects on perceptions of message quality in regulative communication situations. *Human Communication Research, 14,* 68–92.

O'Keefe, B. J., & Shepherd, G. J. (1987). The pursuit of multiple objectives in face-to-face persuasive interactions: Effects of construct differentiation on message organization. *Communication Monographs, 54,* 396–419.

O'Keefe, D. J. (1977). Two concepts of argument. Journal of the american Forensic Association, *13,* 121–128.

O'Keefe, D. J. (1982). The concepts of argument & arguing. In J. R. Cox & C. A. Willard (Eds.), *Advances in argumentation theory & research* (pp. 3–23). Carbondale, IL: Southern Illinois University Press.

Oxford English Dictionary. (1972). *The Compact Edition.* Oxford: Oxford University Press.

Perelman, C. (1979). *The new rhetoric and the humanities.* Dordrecht, Holland: Reidel.

Perelman, C. (1982). *The realm of rhetoric.* Notre Dame, Indiana: University of Notre Dame Press.

Perelman, C., & Ollbrechts-Tyteca L. (1969). *The new rhetoric*. Notre Dame, IN: University of Notre Dame Press. (Original work published 1958)

Popper, K. R. (1979). *Objective knowledge: An evolutionary approach*. (Rev. ed.). Oxford: Oxford University Press.

Quine, W. V. O., & Ullian, J. S. (1970). *The web of belief*. New York: Random House.

Rescher, N. (1964). *Hypothetical reasoning*. Amsterdam: North-Holland Publishers.

Rescher, N. (1967). *Studies in Arabic philosophy*. Pittsburgh: University of Pittsburgh Press.

Rescher, N. (1977). *Dialectics: A controversy-oriented approach to the theory of knowledge*. Albany, NY: SUNY Press.

Rhodes, J., & Newell, S. (Eds.). (1980). *Proceedings of the summer conference on argumentation*. Annandale, VA: American Forensic Association / Speech Communication Association.

Tannen, D. (1990). *You just don't understand*. New York: Ballantine.

Tarski, A. (1965). *Introduction to logic*. New York.: Galaxy.

Toulmin, S. (1969). *The uses of argument*. Cambridge: Cambridge University Press.

Tracy, K. (1984). The effect of multiple goals on conversational relevance and topic shift. *Communication Monographs, 51*, 274–287.

Tracy, K. (1991). *Understanding face to face interaction: Issues linking goals and discourse*. Hillsdale, NJ: Lawrence Erlbaum Associates.

Tracy, K. (1991a). Introduction: linking goals with discourse. In K. Tracy (Ed.), *Understanding face to face interaction: Issues linking goals and discourse* (pp. 1–13). Hillsdale, NJ: Lawrence Erlbaum Associates.

Tracy, K., & Coupland, N. (1990). Multiple goals in discourse: an overview of issues. In K. Tracy & N. Coupland (Eds.), *Multiple goals in discourse* (pp. 1–14). Avon, England: Multilingual Matters Ltd.

Tronto, J. C. (1987.) Beyond gender difference to a theory of care. *Signs, 12*(4), 644–663.

Waldron, V. R., Cegala, D. J., Sharkey, W. F., & Teboul, B. (1990). Cognitive and tactical dimensions of conversational goal management. In K. Tracy & N. Coupland (Eds.), *Multiple goals in discourse* (pp. 101–118). Avon, England: Multilingual Matters Ltd.

Walton, D. N. (1989). Dialogue theory for critical thinking. *Argumentation, 3*(2), 169–184.

Walton, D. N. (1990) What is reasoning? What is an argument? *Journal of Philosophy, LXXXVII*, 399–419.

Walton, D. N. (1992). *The place of emotion in argument*. University Park, PA: The Pennsylvania State University Press.

Warren, K. (1988). Critical thinking and feminism. *Informal Logic, 10*(1), 31–44.

Weimer, W. B. (1983). Why all knowing is rhetorical. *Journal of the American Forensic Associates, 20*(2), 63–71.

Wenzel, J. (1980). Perspectives on argument. In J. Rhodes & S. Newell (Eds.), *Proceedings of the [1979] Summer conference on Argumentation*. Annandale, VA: Speech Communication Association.

Willard, C. A. (1978). A reformulation of the concept of argument: The constructivisit/interactionist foundations of a sociology of argument. *Journal of the American Forensic Association, 14*, 121–140.

Willard, C. A. (1981). The status of the non-discursiveness thesis. *Journal of the American Forensic Association, 17*, 191–214.

Willard, C. A. (1983). *Argumentation and the social grounds of knowledge*. Tuscaloosa, Alabama: University of Alabama Press.

Willard, C. A. (1989). *A theory of argumentation*. Tuscaloosa, Alabama: University of Alabama Press.

Index